THE ULTIMATE DOG PARENT PLAYBOOK

Steps for Feeding, Health & Everyday Care

Table of Contents:

LEGAL NOTICE:

1. Understanding ingredients

Understanding the ingredients of your dog's food items is a must for the dog lovers or dog owners. Whenever you feed the dog with different kinds of food items, you should always read the label and understand the contents about the dog feed types that are being used in such commercial preparations. You should understand the ingredients while buying food for your dog and also know what to look for.

Feed items include dry and fresh food. The fresh dog food that is prepared in homes generally consists of ingredients like freshly cut chicken pieces in addition to the cranberry juices, blue-green algae, etc.

If you come across any different kinds of preservatives and if the dog develops all of a sudden signs pertaining to the food allergy, suspect the unwanted ingredient in the feed items given. Similarly, understand about the moisture status. If the food item is having more moisture, then the dog may prefer this as well.

Beet pulp, pasta, Soy bean oil, wheat middlings, calcium carbonate, magnesium oxide, copper sulphate, iron sulphate, zinc oxide, choline chloride, etc. are often the ingredients in case of vegetarian based diet items offered to the pet animals like dogs.

Raw egg, chicken, beef, mutton, fish, quail etc. are often the preferred ingredients in case of dog diets that are prepared on the basis of the non-vegetarian items. Taurine is one of the essential ingredients for the dog's nutrition. Like wise, in the case of dogs feed with frozen fish items, the vitamin called thiamine needs to be supplemented as an ingredient.

Many premium type of dog food preparations contain essential fatty acids, carbohydrates with adequate fiber contents, vitamins like A, D, E and B complex vitamins.

Furthermore, minerals like zinc, is an essential ingredient for skin health status and calcium, which is an essential ingredient for bone growth, tonicity of muscles. They should be enriched in these food items. However, the cost of those food preparations are comparatively more expensive than the food preparations with general ingredients. Though it may be better for your dog's health.

2. Dogs need different diets at different ages

Dogs need different diets at different ages. Yes. This is true. For example, the puppy needs milk as the major food item while an adult dog may need beef or chicken in addition to the boiled egg and milk. So depending on the age factor, the diet schedule varies in reality for the dogs like any other species.

Puppies need greater amounts of protein, fat and carbohydrates than an adult dogs. Furthermore, puppies need more frequent feeding schedules in a day, unlike an adult dog. The movement based requirements of diet are more in the case of puppies, since they are often more active than the adult dogs.

Elder dogs need restricted protein but the protein needs to be easily digestible and easily assimilated in the body. The diet schedule should have ample supply of water for them. Feeding aged dogs too much protein may finally lead to over burden to the renal structures and ultimately, the dog may end up damaging filters in the kidney.

This is true especially when the immune system of these dogs is compromised due to many factors. Similarly, the elderly dogs need less food only because the movements of the adult dogs are highly restricted and hence, they have to spend a limited of energy. Female dogs in the pregnancy stage need not be fed a full stomach since it may cause some discomforts to the animal. However, the pregnant animal and the nursing animal need special type of food items that deliver a balanced type of nutrition with proper supplementation of vitamins and minerals.

The nursing animal with puppies need to be fed with enough amounts of calcium and hence, there will not be any calcium based deficiency and the bones of the puppies will be strong without any curving.

3. Vitamin and mineral supplements

Vitamin andmineral supplements are the mostimportant components in any dog's feeding. Ifthere is abalancein thevitamin and mineralsupplements,thentheanimalwillhaveahealthylifeand hence,the immunity is not compromised in an unwantedway. This simplymeans thatthere the dog will be more diseaseresistance against various diseases.

Pet owners should know that vitamins A,D, E,andK arethe fat-soluble vitamins and others are water-soluble vitamins. Vitamins like thiamine,pyridoxine and cyanocobalaminare important forthe functions of nervous system. Deficiencyof vitamin Aleads tonight blindness and skin lesions and deficiencyof vitamin Dleads tothe softeningandweakeningof the bones.

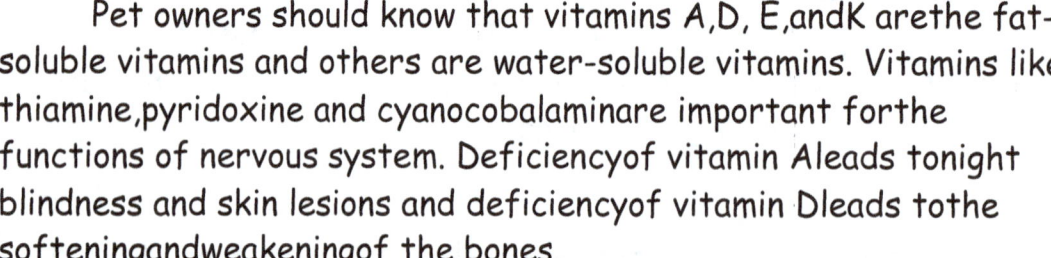

These problems are many atime encountered by the dog owners. Amongthese, vitamin Atoxicities mayoccurifyoufeed themin excessive amounts, likevitamin D. Hence,give emphasis on this while you areusingthesevitaminsinthedogs.Codliveroilfromselected fishes has morevitamin A inthem and are universally good feed for dogs.

All dogs may not needsupplements of minerals orvitamins tolive well forthemoment,butitisimportantfortheirfuture.Ifthey becomesick or aged or very youngwithoutproper feeding, supplementations arerequired forthe upkeepof healthstatus in them. However, one has to followthe instructions ofveterinarian in this regard.

If the dogs are fed with fishin frozen conditions, then theymay be sufferingconstantlyfromvitaminB1deficiencyandhence,such dogs need to be given specificallyB1. Careless supplementations of minerals maylead to diseases and hence,veterinarians always needto be consultedonthesupplementationofmineralsorvitamins.

Minerals like calcium, magnesium, zinc, manganese, iron, copper etc. are given more emphasis in addition to sodium and potassium. Zinc isrelated to skin health and potassium is related to the muscle health and calcium with phosphorus is related to the bone health.

However, if you feed the dog with chicken, mutton or beef along with required vegetables, artificial supplementation of mineral or vitamin tablets may be highly reduced but supplements need to be thought of when you are not able to maintain a balanced nutrition as this happens with most of the dogs, due to multifaceted causes.

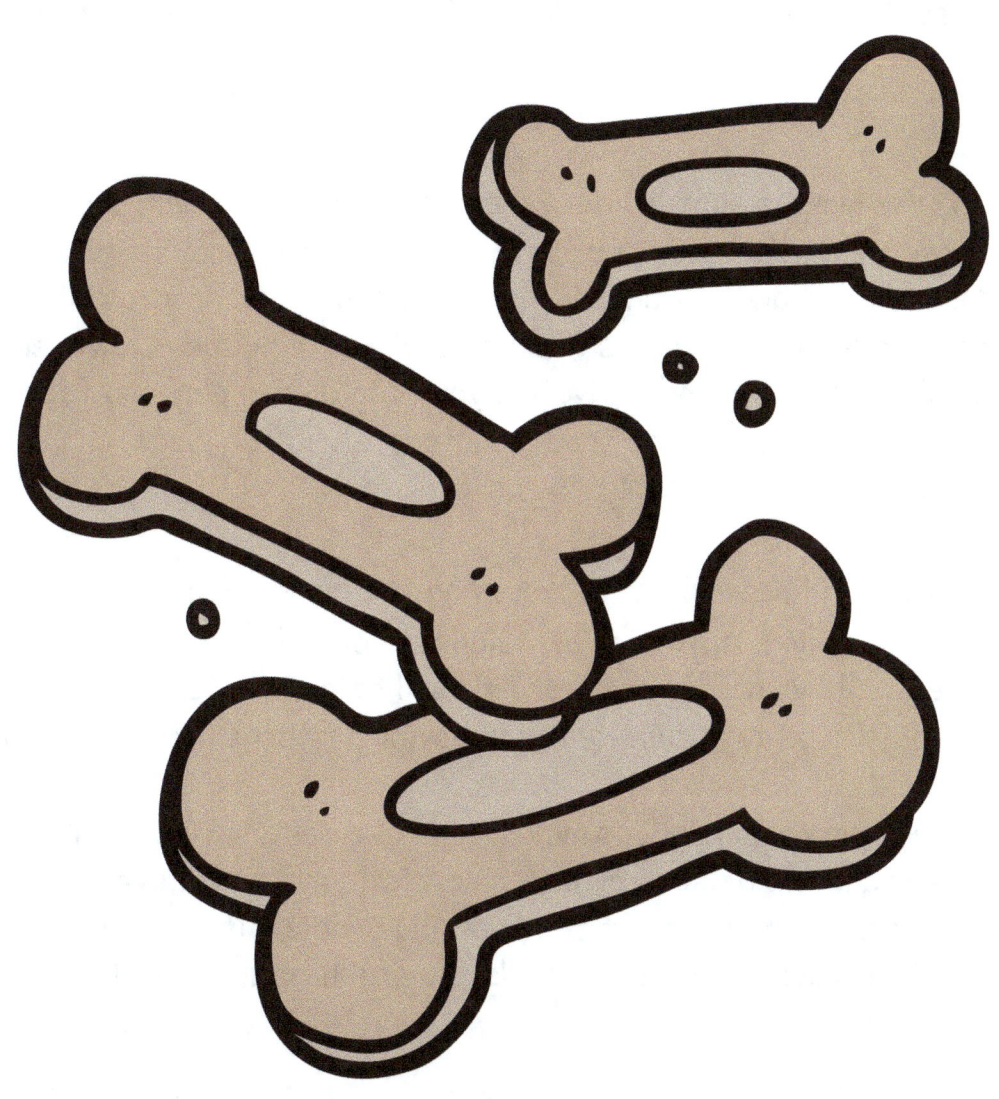

4. Boredom and variety

Boredom and variety are always inter connected in case of dog misbehaving. Yes. This is true. Many a times, boredom can be managed with variety of materials that will distract the animals to a greater extent. Hence, the dog may not do the abnormal or unwanted activity arising out of the boredom experienced by it.

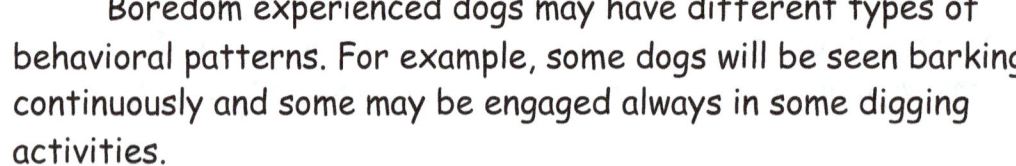

Boredom experienced dogs may have different types of behavioral patterns. For example, some dogs will be seen barking continuously and some may be engaged always in some digging activities.
There are many ways to get your dog out of its boredom activities. Many toys are available which simulated duck, dog, rodent etc.

These may be kept inside the crate and in particular, puppies love these items. A buster cube with multiple treats may be placed in the dog's shelter and the animal soon understands on how to roll the buster cube to get the treats it prefers. A Buster Cube is an ingenious toy use for simulating and activating your dog during play and feed time. Instead of placing the food monotonously in one place, change the place of feeding suddenly.

Such actions will be helpful for removing the boredom like activity in your dog. Activities pertaining to boredom need to be redefined well by the dog owners. This will help them to a greater extent to drive away the unwanted behavior patterns in their pet dogs.

For example, some dogs may often have destructive biting characters and will be seen biting chair, cloth, mats, and everything that can see. After ruling out the teething problem if it is a puppy, provide it with some large sized balls, mineral mixture based bone materials, etc. Such variety of materials help to reduce the boredom related activities.

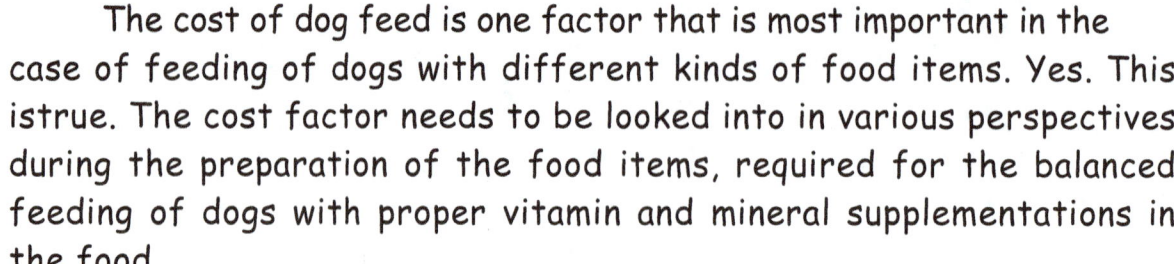

The cost of dog feed is one factor that is most important in the case of feeding of dogs with different kinds of food items. Yes. This istrue. The cost factor needs to be looked into in various perspectives during the preparation of the food items, required for the balanced feeding of dogs with proper vitamin and mineral supplementations in the food.

Cost will not always matter much because the dog's value is being assessed in terms of companionship and the happiness derived from the dog to the dog owner. Though the cost of the food items is comparatively more, many dog owners don't mind much due to the increased benefits derived from their dogs in terms of protection, guiding, etc.

Selection of ingredients for the home made food needs to be however based on the quality factor. Even when the quality is more, general persons may seek some cheaper items only. Recommended nutrient contents may be obtained from the national nutrient academies in all nations and this will provide guidelines.

One can correlate the cost factor with items available in their own country. Generally, the commercial food items are expensive especially the ones that use the modern technologies of food preparation like oven-baking, sterilization of cans, air drying or freeze drying of contents etc.

Canned items cost more than the dry food items. However, the cost of the items depends on what kind of food item to be used for the dogs. Food allergies need to be monitored during usage of different food items in case of dogs due to the cheaper cost of the items. Often the quality need not be compromised because of the cost factor.

Most of the dog food items nowadays have mentioned their cost in the label itself. Hence, the dog owner need not have any problem in taking a decision on the purchase.

6. Dry vs. Canned food

These types of food materials are different with different grades of liking by the dogs. Dogs like dry foods only if they are tasty only and however, on comparison, the dogs prefer only the canned food items. Reason for such preference by the dogs is that in case of canned food items, the moisture is about seventy to eighty per cent but in case of dry food, it is only about ten per cent.

However, if you view it in terms of nutrients, often the dry food contains nearly ninety per cent nutrients whereas the canned food items contain only less per cent of nutrients and most of the times. It is only soy products that are structured so well to look like meat pieces.

Hence, to make up the nutritional balance in the body systems, the dog has to eat more amounts of canned food materials than the dry food materials. Hence, just compare the cost factor related to this feature by you. Many dry food items are soybean and rice based.

Now some dry food items are based on corn. Sometimes, beef based or chicken based food items come in the cans along with mineral and vitamin supplements suited for the upkeep of the dog's health status. Larger dogs that weigh more than thirty pounds need to be fed with semi moist food items or dry food items in most of the occasions.

This is to satisfy the food receptors in the stomach. This is due to the fact that the larger dogs need to eat plenty of moist food or the canned food items to satisfy these criteria. But it may not be practically possible in these larger dogs. The small sized dogs may have a satisfactory level of nutrients if fed even the moist food items. However, the caloric density of the dry food should not be forgotten. Enriched dry food items are highly welcome ones than the non - enriched food items.

7. Home made diets

Home made diets are important in the dog feeding. Many a times, the commercial diets consist of food items that have artificial coloring agents and flavoring agents that are harmful to the dog's body. Home made food items have the guarantee of freshness in the preparation unlike the ready-made commercial items.

The preservatives added in the commercial food items may not be the suitable ones to the dogs from the health point of view. Even in case of renal diseases in dogs, the home made diets may be made with ground beef, slices of bread, calcium carbonate, boiled eggs etc.

The purpose is to have the restricted protein supply in the feed items prepared. This should be carried out with home made diets prepared exclusively for the dogs suffering from renal diseases. Water is added in sufficient quantities to help the proper metabolism in the digestion-impaired renal cases.

The dog may have allergic symptoms like severe itching, which may not get corrected by different kinds of medications employed over a period of time. Such cases may get easily treated once the dog food is changed from the commercial type of food to the home made food items.

Often, the home made food items are prepared using the freezing procedures to kill the germs or by adding grape seed extracts to provide sufficient antioxidants to the home made food items. Food grade vinegar is also added in many times to the meat pieces prepared in a fresh manner. All these can be enriched with vitamin supplements that are available in fruit essences, fish oil etc.

Cranberry juice, bananas, fish and meat are prepared in a quality manner and no preservatives are added during the preparation of these kinds of food items and the dog becomes more active after the consumption of such food items.

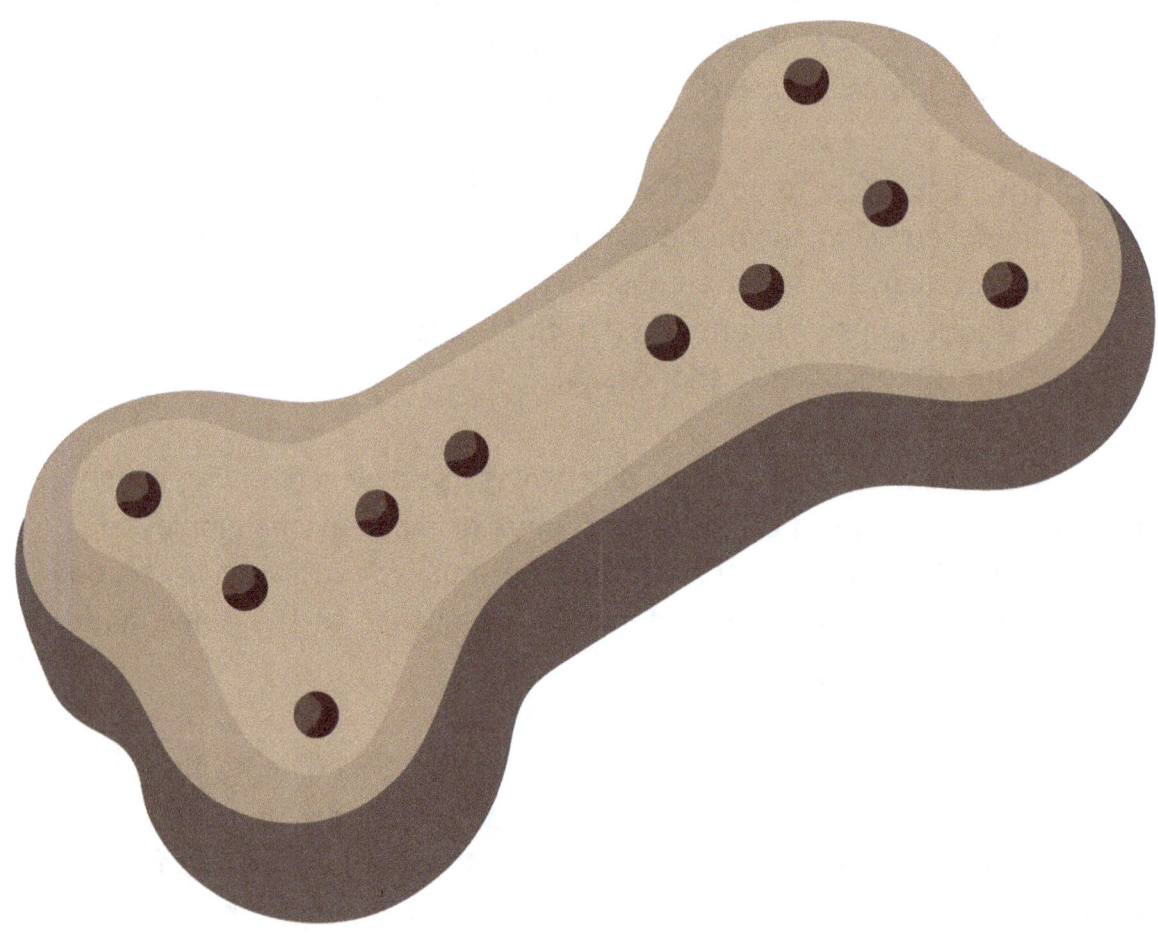

8. Food allergies

Food allergies are something that is difficult to identify unless one is well aware of the baseline information with regard to this type of allergy. The main symptoms of food allergies in dogs include the facial itching, limb chewing, belly itching, recurrent ear infections or skin infections.

Since the dogs consume lot of prepared food materials including various kinds of proteins, fillers, coloring agents and more; in the commercial food materials, the incidences of food allergies are more than one can imagine. Allergic reactions mostly involve the skin or the gastro intestinal tract.

If you come across your dog itching after the provision of specific food materials, then suspect the food allergy in this animal. However, conditions like fungal infections need to be ruled out in general before the conclusion of itching as a sign of food allergy.

There are many recorded incidences of allergies of dogs to corn or to wheat. However, the food allergies vary from dog to dog. Read the labels clearly before feeding your dogs with pet food materials, in such occasions. Too much colored food materials may be avoided since they may cause allergies to your dog.

Food allergies are often linked to the hyper active behavior noticed in the dogs. Added colors, preservatives, and high fat diet might cause such food allergies in the dogs and hence, one has to be careful in providing new kind of diet to their dogs and closely monitor the dog for any signs of allergy.

There are many occasions that food allergies might be diagnosed in the dogs but the dog may have other problems like pancreatitis. To rule out the food allergies, observation your dogs everytime you feed them, look for reasons to link the signs of dog with food given, specific signs encountered, differential diagnosis etc. are the important features to be given emphasis.

9. How much should I feed my dog?

Many people will give different types of answers based on their experience with their dogs. However, the scientific facts related to the feeding aspects in case of dogs need to be given emphasis during the feeding activities maintained in case of dogs.

Usually the puppies should not be separated before they are eight weeks old. However, some times the orphaned puppies may exist. Usually about five percent of the body weight may be taken as criteria for the quantity of food to be given to the puppies. However, the amount that is consumed by the dog varies with size of the dogs also.

However, one can have a thumb rule of feeding the puppy goes until you see visible fullness of the abdomen to a moderate degree. If you are going on feeding the animal without giving emphasis to the animal's stomach appearance, then the puppy may experience some kinds of digestive upsets and the diarrhea may occur in them.

This may cause many inconveniences to the owner as well as the puppy. Unlike adult dogs, the puppies need to be fed with restricted amounts of food but in more frequencies. However, once the age advances, the amount may be increased to some extent but the frequency of feeding is often decreased in many occasions.

A dog on a raw diet may consume only two to four percent of their body weight. Just observe closely the feeding pattern of the dog and the body condition of the animal. If the dog becomes obese, just reduce the quantity of food and if the dog becomes thin, then have an increase in the feeding items.

As mentioned earlier, puppies and adolescent dogs eat more than the adult dogs. Likewise the geriatric dog eats less than the adult dog due to the reduced movements of the dog. However, remember to restrict the amounts of protein during the feeding of diet to the aged dogs.

10. How often should I feed my dog?

This often becomes an important question asked by many dog lovers and dog owners. If it is a puppy within age of the first six weeks, the puppies need to be given milk at the rate of five to seven times per day. The puppy will make some sound if it wants to feed in general.

However, the feeding frequency may be reduced when the dog becomes six to eight weeks old. By the time the dog assumes the age of four weeks, it may start taking of some solid food. Hence, mix the solid food with water in majority and feed your puppy once or twice in the beginning and if the dog develops some diarrhea, then delay the feeding.

Most of the times, it is due to trial and error but taking some basic steps in feeding, so you need to watch out. The feeding frequency may be changed to two to three times after the assumption of age of eight weeks. However, if the dog is seen hungry craving for food, then provide food once than the estimated numbers. This varies with different breeds of dogs.

However, avoid feeding too many times in this age group of dogs. Around three months to six months of age, the puppy will be teething. Hence, restrict the feeding to two times only but the balanced type of nutrition needs to be provided to the dogs of this age group to avoid the deficiency based symptoms in them.

From six months to one year, try using puppy food that is available commercially. However, from first year onwards, the adult food may be given gradually. However, when the dog becomes an elder dog, restrict the frequency of feeding since the movements of such adult dogs are highly reduced due to multiple reasons. However, the pregnant animal may be fed an extra time depending on the willingness of the animal and restrict the quantity of the food but without compromising on the quality of food.

11. Signs of Ill health

Signs of ill health are the most important signs of the health status in your dogs. For example, if the dog has continuous nasal discharge, it indicates the presence of nasal congestion and if the discharge is thick, most of the times, the dog may have pneumonia.

If the dog vomits one or two times occasionally, this may not be taken as a serious sign of ill health but if the dog continues this vomiting, then this is something significant to be looked into.

If the dog has continuous itching, then one needs to check up the dog first by closer observation and examination of skin by separating the hair material especially in case of long haired breeds. You may also come across a lot of ticks or lice on skin, which may look apparently normal at a distance.

If the dog passes loose stool for one or two times, this need not be given more emphasis but if there is continuous passing of loose stool, then the dog is understood to suffer from bowel disorders. If the dog does not pass stool for two to three days, the digestive upsets needs to be ruled out carefully.

Just patiently observe the dog's walking movements and rule out any abnormal movements in the dog. If the dog is limping, the animal may have foot lesions. Similarly, if the aged dog has reluctant walking and less feed intake along with repeated vomiting, then acute renal disorders like nephritis needs to be ruled out.

If there is whiteness in eyes, suspect the corneal opacity that may occur in diseases like trypanasomosis. When the dog becomes anemic, the mucous membrane of the eyes becomes paler and in severe cases, this may have wall white color. If the dog bites chain and owners or others, look for behavior disorders and rabies needs to be ruled out.

12. Heart worm, fleas and other parasites

Heart worm, fleas andother parasites in dogsneed tobe eliminated by followingappropriate medications in them. Many products have come up in the commercialfields toprotect the dogs from heartworms,fleasandotherparasiteslikehookworms,whip worms, round worms, lice, ticks etc.

Amongthe heart worm, fleas andother parasites, the fleas producethe hyper sensitivereactions in the affected animals. Hence, the animalsinfestedwithfleasstartseverelyscratchingofbody. Many times,thescratchingissosevereandtheskinbecomesmore hyperemic and dermatitis occurs inthe affectedareas.

Animal will not lie down orsleep comfortably dueto the constant bites bythefleas.Hence,animallooksasifaffectedbysomesevere skin disease.Iftheanimalisnotproperlyattendedforthistickbite problem, there will beoften secondary bacterialinvasions in these sites andtheremayevenbeabadsmellemanatingfromtheskinareas.

Closeobservation of the dog ishighly essential torule out the occurrenceof fleas disturbingthe animaltoa greaterextent. Similarly, theskin of the animalneeds tobetestedforthe presence of ticks,liceetc.Forthis,thehairmaterialsneedtobeseparatedand the closeobservationwithpatienceisrequiredfortheproper diagnosis.

In many incidences, ifanemia is present,the blood protozoa need toberuledoutinadditiontothehookwormproblems.The clinical problems likeanemia, loosemotion,pot bellyetc. might be recognized bythe dogowners themselvesand however, the dog needs to undergotheroutinehealthrelatedexaminationinvolvingfecal examination, hematological examination and bloodsmear examination.

Many commercial products have come up in the market, which are useful to deal with all these conditions by single dose. Drugs like ivermectin are highly useful and are available in both injection and oral form in addition to the solution form that can be applied on the skin. These drugs in dogs can lead to the prophylaxis of these conditions also.

13. Heart worm prevention

Beef flavored chunks are available in addition to the beef flavored tablets or solutions that can be given orally to the dogs as a measure against the incidence of heart worms. Avoid mosquito bites by providing proper mosquito-proof shelter facilities to the dogs.

Just plan whether there is any need to go for the heart worm prevention though out the year or only in some months of the year. For example, in case of some countries, the mosquitoes may be dormant in most of the colder months.

However, in some countries, this is not a position. Many a times, medications are available for oral administration to prevent heart worms along with hookworms etc. Such oral medications need to be taken as per the instructions. However, be cautious about the occurrence of any adverse drug reactions in the dog given with such prophylactic therapy.

Adverse event reports need to be sent if you come across any sorts of adverse drug reactions in your dog during the preventive treatment.
Soft beef flavored tablets are highly preferred by the pet animals as the preventive measure against heart worms. The pet owner needs to consult a veterinarian if the dose for the prophylaxis of heart worm is missed for few months. In such occasions, the pet animal needs to undergo the heart worm test.

Heartgard, sentinel, interceptor, revolution, etc. are available in the commercial fields as drugs for the preventive measure. Avoid water stagnation around the dog shelter and the bushes around the area that facilitate mosquito breeding. This test needs to be carried out in consultation with a veterinarian who is specialized in the pet animal health care and medicine.

As a preventive measure for the heart worms, the dogs need to be tested for the evidence of these worms at an age of six months. Real beef chew able tablets are available containing medical agent like ivermectin.

14. Common questions about heart worm

The common questions about heart worm are often related to the species affected by heart worms in addition to the dogs. One should know that in addition to dogs, the cat, fox, wolf, horse, sea lion etc. are also affected. Can this be cured or not? Yes. This can be treated.

What is the drug used often for the prevention of heart worm in dogs? Ivermectin is the drug used often to have preventive actions for these heart worms. Dogs affected reveal constant coughing, panting and dullness in many occasions.

What will be the size of the worms? In the case of the females, it is about twenty-seven centimeters and in the case of males, it is about seventeen centimeters in length. Is there any vector involve in the transmission of the disease? Yes. Mosquitoes often get associated as
vectors in which the early development of larvae of heart worms occur in them.

Is the prophylaxis meant only for heart worms or others also? The prophylaxis is meant not only for the heart worms but also for the hook worms, whip worms, and round worms. What is the infective type of larvae that is associated with the transmission of these heart worms? The third stage larva that is transmitted by the mosquito bites.

This occurs through out the world. In some areas, the incidences are less in colder months in which the mosquito breeding will not be there and may be dormant during these periods. What is the name of the drug used for therapy and prevention? Ivermectin and milbemycin oxime may be used for both purposes. Ivermectin is available in injection form and oral form.

Additionally, the forms for external application are also available. The cost factor needs to be worked out for all these treatments. What is the frequency of drug used for prophylaxis? One month before the mosquito season and up to two months after the mosquito season, ivermectin or milbemycin oxime may be given once monthly for the prophylaxis. Diethylcarbamazine may be used for therapy purpose.

15. Fleas and other parasites

Fleas and other parasitesneed tobegiven always apriorityby the dogowners.Thecommonincidencesoffleabiteallergyincaseof dogs causeworriesamongthedogowners.Fleabiteinducesallergic reactions in the concerned area bitten bythefleas. Hence, the affectedarea looks like hairless area andthe animalstarts scratching.

Fleas cause severe dermatitis in dogswithsevereflea infestations. Many times, theflea bite causes allergicreactions in the dogs. In manyoccasions, dogsexperiencesevere discomforts dueto these allergic reactions. Medicated collars are availableto treat and prevent theinfestation withexternalparasites like ticks orfleas.

Other parasites like ticks, lice inaddition tothe internal parasites like hook worms, round worms,whip worms etc. cause affections in the healthstatusofthe animal. Forexample, if hookworm affects the animal, mostofthetimes,the dog hasanemia. Theanemicsigns become moreprominentdepending on the degreeof affection bythe hookworm.

Hookworm larvae can pass directlythrough theskinand cause problems in the affectedones. Such dogs mayreveallesions pertaining to thedermatitisinthefeetregionandintheskinareas.Skinrashes may beseen frequentlyin such casesandthe affected animalpasses loosestool, which is of redtinged and mixed with bloodmaterial.

If theroundworms areseen in morenumbers,the affected puppies reveal a potbellycondition, whichis easily recognizedbythe dog ownersthemselves.Piperazinesaltsaregivenbyoralrouteforthe treatment of this problem. However, broad-spectrum anthelmintics like pyrantelpamoate,fenbendazoleetc.aregiventotreatthese conditions.

Many drugs have come in market to treat the fleas and other parasites. Nowadays, the medical agent called as ivermectin is highly preferred by many dog owners to treat the fleas and other parasites in dogs. This drug is available in injection form and oral form. Even the drug is available for the external application also.

16. Do parasites cause "Scooting"?

Parasites too cause the scooting. Scooting is a an anal sac disease. First let's understand what scooting is in detail. This is the dragging of anus with the hind limbs in an extended state. Parasites causing irritation in the anus regions lead to such type of actions in animals like dogs.

However, one should not be under the impression that it is the parasite that alone causes such scooting in case of dogs. There are many occasions in which the dog may have the scooting without any parasite based etiological agent. For example, the anal gland infections, tumors at the anus and injuries near the anal regions also may lead to such type of dragging of anus region, frequently by the affected dogs.

Flea bite allergy often causes irritation at the anus region and the animal may try to bite the anus region and the irritations due to these factors lead to the final dragging of anus region on the ground. Cestodiasis in dogs is the condition caused by tapeworms.

In such occasions, if the animal is not treated in time, the animal may be seen exhibiting the scooting activities. Tapeworm segments passed in the stool create crawling like activities near anus.

Such crawling activities of the tapeworm segments lead to severe itching at these regions. Hence, to make a relief from this type of constant irritation, the animal starts pressing the anus region on the ground first and then tries to drag it on the ground with typical extension of rear limbs.

Usually there is a packet of eggs when the fecal sample is examined by microscope. However, the flotation technique leads to breakage of these packets to burst and hence, diagnosis is difficult in such occasions. Scooting dogs need to be examined to rule out tapeworm segments, which look like rice like pieces.

These segments are white in color and turn yellow when taken from the body. Tapeworms themselves may be seen in the motion or near anus below the tail regions. Consult your veterinarian for specific cures for this.

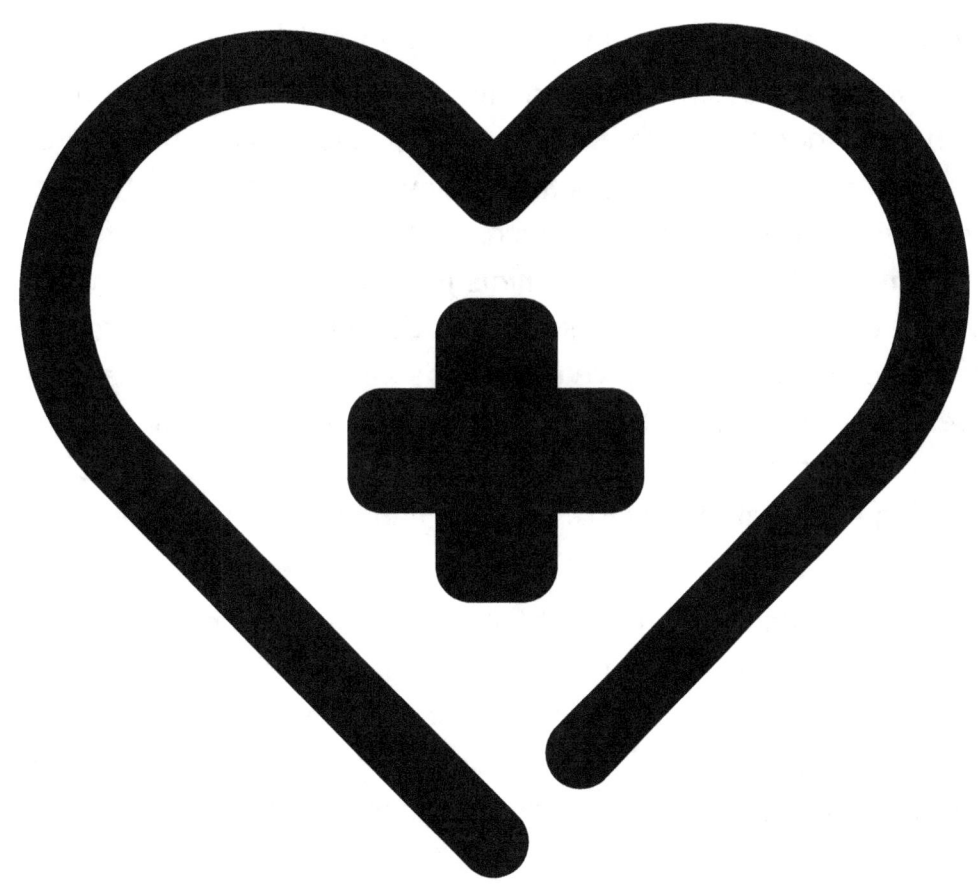

17. Preventing dental disease

Preventing dental disease is an important feature, which is to be paid more emphasis by the dog lovers or dog owners. Dental disease is given priority in the health schedule of the dog nowadays because of the association of the dental diseases with systemic diseases in the dogs.

Antibiotics need to be given in the initial stage of teeth infection itself and if not, this may cause specific infections and the organisms may spread to the other nearby regions like the oral mucous membrane and pharyngeal region etc.

More acidic or alkaline food materials need not be given to the dogs to avoid the possible teeth damage. Antibiotics need to be given in the initial stage of teeth infection itself and if not, this may cause specific infections and the organisms may spread to the other nearby regions like the oral mucous membrane and pharyngeal region etc. More acidic or alkaline food materials need not be given to the dogs to avoid the possible teeth damage. If the dog is not given at its young age some bony material to bite on, the dog may develop some dental diseases later. The teething action often causes the animal to go for biting in an indiscriminate manner. Hence, the animal has to be given some biting materials to avoid the occurrence of dental diseases.

If there is an evidence of bleeding from the oral region, the dog needs to be examined thoroughly for any dental abnormality. Mainly the puppies or some times, the adult dogs also may have teeth injuries. They need to be attended immediately as a preventive step. If not, the animal may end up in secondary bacterial infections.

Hunting dogs need additional care associated with the dental structures and such care is needed to avoid the future dental problems in such dogs. Brushes are available to provide better dental care to dogs. However, one has to allot more time and should have patience to use such brushes in case of dogs.   This may lead into further problems. Centers for disease control and prevention are trying to put up guidelines to prevent the dental diseases in dogs in many nations. However, the oral examination needs to be carried out frequently in dogs and such activities help to rule out the emerging problems pertaining to the dentine structures in the beginning itself.

18. Home dental care

Home dental care is to be given more emphasis nowadays because of the fact that the dental diseases are emerging in the case of pet animals like dogs to a greater extent. Though you are giving home dental care, if you suspect on the extension of the dental diseases, then immediately approach the veterinarian for intervention.

Try to provide bone materials without very sharp points to the dogs and they may love to chew them and then swallow the bitten products. Such activities help them to go for the development of strong teeth structures in a natural manner.

Mind that the breeds of dogs like Pekingese, etc. are more prone for the development of teeth diseases because the teeth are closely crowned in the oral cavity be to the small size of the these dogs. Hence, these dogs need to be checked up for the excessive plaque formation in the home itself.

Recreational raw beef bones are wonderful materials to keep the teeth structures of your dog clean and free from formation of plaque with build up of bacterial organisms. Teeth brushes are available for use with care in case of dogs and one has to be careful during the usage of these brushes in dogs. Teeth brushes are to be used with special kinds of pastes recommended by the veterinarians for home use in case of dogs.

Specially prepared food materials are available in the pet shops to remove the tartar and the plaque materials from the teeth structures. Dry dog food and toys that are specially made to add strength to the teeth structures are often used at home for better teeth cleaning.

The plaque materials are intermittently to be removed at home to avoid any occurrence of the periodontal diseases, which are more common among the dogs. Dental wipes are available in the pet shops and they may be used carefully in the home. This helps to remove more plaque and the tartar like materials that are loosely attached.

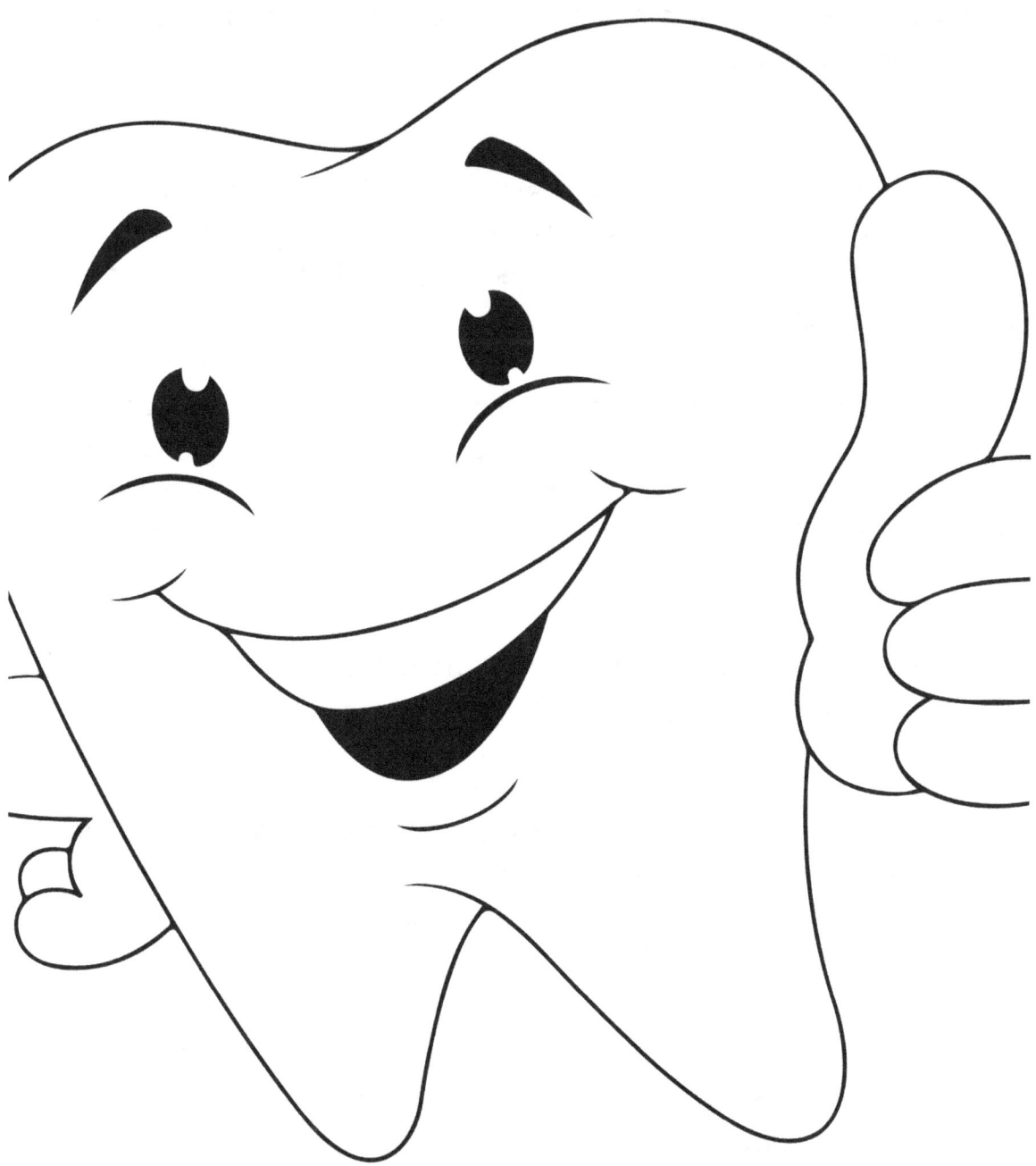

19. Veterinary dental treatments

Veterinary dental treatments are more important. If the dental structures are not being looked carefully, there are more chances for the development of periodontal diseases in dogs. Hence, the veterinary dental treatments need to be paid maximum importance during the life of your dogs.

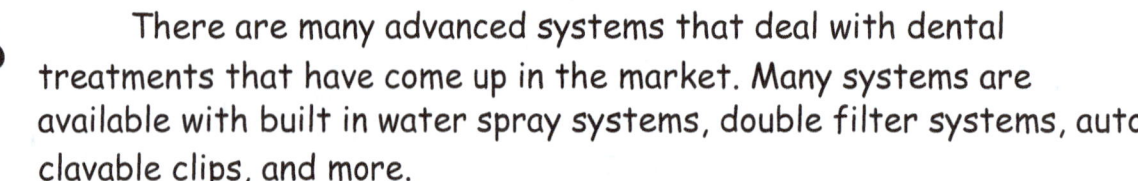

There are many advanced systems that deal with dental treatments that have come up in the market. Many systems are available with built in water spray systems, double filter systems, auto clavable clips, and more.

Many veterinarians use high speed fiber optic hand pieces with push button turbines, two hand piece water jet systems, soundless water compressors and more. The diagnosis of a condition pertaining to the periodontal structure based diseases are more important before the treatment.

Periodontal diseases are graded into minimal and moderate and severe diseases. Accordingly the therapy is carried out, it is impossible to check all teeth by basic oral examination in the dog patient. Hence, general anesthesia is required before the examination of the teeth inside structures. Surgical curettage is done in case of advanced periodontal diseases using flaps and the teeth extractions are also carried out using moderate force and more care is taken to avoid the continuous bleeding.

Oral surgeries are undertaken after obtaining of the dental radio graphs in the dogs and by comparing the tissue damage with normal teeth structures. The concerned veterinarians assess the extent of damage in a systematic manner.

The periodontal diseases are controlled by administration of broad-spectrum antibiotics in an effective manner. Along with the dental surgeries, the oral treatment is done with many products that are helpful to prevent the attachment of the tartar or plaque on the teeth. However, reputable products should be used in the veterinary practice and the dog owner's satisfaction is given more priority during the veterinary dental therapy.

20. The importance of the physical examination

The importance of the physical examination need not be underestimated in case of dogs. Simple but systematic physical examination techniques may diagnose most of the disorders in dogs and hence, without physical examination of the dog, one should not resort to knowing the status of your dog's health.

Simply observe the dog with scratching. Catch the dog and simply separate the hair material from the itching site. To the surprise you may come across a big wound in the scratched site. The wound might be the main reason for the scratching of the dog at that site. However, one has to rule out the occurrence of wound by severe itching itself.

Many times, when the scratching dog is examined physically, one can come across plenty of lice infestation or tick problem in the skin and coat. The parasitic condition might not be diagnosed at all if one has not carried out the physical examination. Similarly, the dog may reveal the signs of pain when the physical examination is carried out by deep palpation technique. The dog show signs of pain when the dog is examined at the stomach or the back regions.

Even if it is possible that by pressure based palpation, one can detect the acute renal disorders in the affected dogs turn to the examined site at the region of kidney or at the back region. The dog affected by the Cystitis with severe retention of urine is often diagnosed by mere physical examination.

The filled bladder together with signs of pain during the examination at the site of urinary bladder indicates that the animal is affected by Cystitis. Auscultation of the heart in both right and left sides helps to rule out the abnormal heart sounds and the pulmonary area based auscultation reveals the respiratory system disorder like pneumonia.

21. Why are regular check-ups important?

Why are regular check-ups important? Every dog owner asks this type of question, often. If you failed to do the regular check-ups, then the dog may end up having some major diseases that you don't know about. Hence, you need to pay lot of money both to the veterinarians for consultancy and for the required drugs useful for the therapy of the clinical condition.

One may not be able to find out the very commonly occurring clinical conditions in case of their dogs because of less experience with dog diseases or dog rearing. This is why check ups are important. For example, if the dog has potbelly, the condition may not look abnormal many times. But if the dog is subjected to the regular check-up, then the veterinarian immediately finds it out and gives the appropriate therapy. If not, the animal may experience diarrhea and the dehydration.

If the dog has any signs of illness, then don't wait for the regular check-up. Instead, you need to approach the veterinarian immediately. Check ups if done in a regular manner will help to give vaccinations against canine distemper, parvovirus, corona virus, rabies virus, hepatitis virus, and more.

Booster vaccinations will be carried out in such cases without any delay in the injections and this helps to improve the immunity level of the dog against such diseases in a remarkable degree. Regular check up is the essential one with proper stools examination. Hence, the deworming may be carried out with drugs like fenbendazole, albendazole, etc.

Abnormalities like signs of pain may be ruled out during such examinations. If not, helminthiasis may affect the animal and diarrhea may occur in addition to the other types of digestive upsets and anemia. Regular examinations help to rule out the external parasitic conditions like lice or tick infestations. Dental problems are also found outduring the regular check ups in reputed veterinary hospitals.

22. What happens during an examination?

This question often looks so simple but holds more meanings in that. During the examination of your dog, first you need to prepare the dog first psychologically for a better-restrained status. For this, you need to take a leash and place the dog on table by the careful delivery of suitable command.

When the dog is trying to avoid the thorough examination by the veterinarian, just try to distract the dog by simple scratching of your dog behind the ears, etc. Hence, the dog's attention is some what diverted from the examination procedures that are carried out often in a systematic manner.

However, there are obedient dogs, which will remain calm during an examination. Such dogs need to be given some patting on the shoulder or the body and praises. Perhaps, many owners may try to provide some treats that are liked so much by the concerned dogs. However, it all depends on the trainings offered to the concerned dog earlier and the effective follow up procedures by the owner for the maintenance of such reflexes during the examination.

Muzzles are required for some dogs if they behave in a different manner by objecting the examination procedures by the frequent movements of the body or trying to bite the veterinarian doing the examination of the dog. Hence, the owner needs to observe the dog closely during the examination to rule out any abnormal activity by the dog.

Restraining activities in a proper manner during the clinical examination of the dog are of highly appreciable if they are successful with the concerned dogs. Such control will be of highly helpful for the effective examination of the patient by the concerned veterinarian in the pet clinic.

If the dog gets more distracted during examination by means of restlessness, then one may even use the electronic equipments which will make some sound that are audible to the dogs' ear. Such things will be helpful in the proper distraction of the animal during the examination.

23. How often should my pet be examined?

Most of the dog owners try to find this answer in a serious manner. Whatever the schedule we have for the examination of your pet animal, if there is any abnormality noticed in your animal, without delay, you need to subject the animal for a thorough clinical examination. It can be suggested that even before the purchase of a puppy, just consult a pet animal care specialist and try to understand about the schedules to be maintained for the examination of the animal. This will help a lot in solving many health related problems in the concerned animal.

Though once in two or three months is the general schedule for the examination of the dog, as soon as the puppy is procured the dog needs to be taken to the veterinarian for a thorough examination. Hence, the health care measures related program will be obtained in time. Most of the time, the dog is to be taken to the veterinarian at fifth or sixth week of age because in this period only, the vaccinations against diseases will be systematically carried out. The period of vaccination in the first year will be continued up to the sixteenth week of age and the schedule needs to be maintained accordingly.

However, if you have the pregnant dog, the dog need not be stressed by long distance based transportation for examination purposes. Hence, consult the veterinarian by phone and try to reduce the travel for the dog. However, the veterinary advice needs to be obtained in terms of health maintenance. If the dog has met with an accident either during travel or during routine movements, the animal needs to be taken to the pet hospital immediately.

Though no disease is evident, it does not mean that the dog is healthy. There are occasions wherein the animal may look like a normal dog but may have some diseases, which can be found out during the routine health check ups. Hence, the owner has to decide on when to take the dog to the hospital depending on necessity.

24. How to administer medicine

Most of the times, the dogs are so intelligent to find out the drug mixed water or food materials offered to them by the dog owners. Hence, often it becomes a headache for the dog owners to give medicines to their dogs. To the possible extent, the animal need not be forced for taking of the drug. If the medicine is to be given by mouth, first decide whether it is better to give it along with water or food. Many times, the medicines are mixed with food materials and are kept in concealed position by proper mixing of the medicine with the food materials.

Before administering the medicine, just delay the feeding time in the particular dog. Hence, the dog may be hungry to some extent. At that time, give little quantity of normal food without medicine and the dog may eat it well without any suspicion and now provide the medicine mixed food and the dog may voluntarily eat it most of the times. If the dog resists, first restraint the dog well and open the mouth. Place the tablet behind the fang teeth and almost behind the bulb of the tongue. However, take care that the medicine what you are administering in the dog should not enter directly into the respiratory organ like lungs.

If so, the dog will experience many bouts like activities and may end up in aspiration pneumonia with severe nasal discharge and panting like activities. In puppies, just swab the medicine around the upper lip. The puppy will lick automatically the drug by tongue. Hence, the administration becomes perfect in such cases.

If the medicine is in liquid form, don't raise the head of dog too much and place medicine by a syringe. Just by using a dropper, fill the medicine in the lip pocket. The continuous rubbing at the throat side may stimulate the swallowing. Making the animal thirsty and then offering of medicine mixed water may many times help the intake of the medicine.

25. Nursing a sick dog

Nursing a sick dog is one of the vital measures that a dog owner needs to understand. Similarly, when a dog becomes sick, the dog is in need of more care and affection based activities by the dog owners. Nursing a sick animal is often considered as an art and this should not be taken as a causal measure.

Yes. You need to take extra care to the dog when it becomes sick. For example, the sick dog with high fever needs to be given only some bread pieces and bulky non-vegetarian items may be avoided. Such dogs should be kept in some calm place after medications are taken and should not be disturbed. During the nursing of the dog who has taken the drug, the animal needs coaxing and stroking by the owner. Don't raise the dog's head too much to avoid the passing of drugs given by the mouth directly into the respiratory organs like lungs. During the nursing measures, take care by giving warm fluids.

Safety is to be given more priority during the nursing activity in any dog. When the dog has severe diarrhea, the animal may start showing signs of dehydration. Hence, the nursing care for dehydration includes an addition of small doses of salt and glucose to water in a careful manner.
Similarly, the vomiting dog also needs proper nursing care. Ice cubes may be given in such cases along with egg whites to smooth the esophageal passage.

Nowadays, a non-contact based infrared thermometer has come upinthemarket to obtain the temperature of the animal without much stress.Place the dog in a shaded place if the temperature is so high andprovide good ventilation to the suffering animal. If the animal is sufferingfrom hypothermia, provide warm blankets to given comfort totheanimal.

26. Vaccinations

Vaccinations need to be undertaken always by the pet owners and the dogs need to be vaccinated at the appropriate time. This helps to improve the resistance of the animal against some specific diseases causing frequently problems in dogs. The dogs that are orphaned due to the death of the mother have lesser protection in their immune system. Such animals are to be particularly protected against various diseases.

Vaccination is usually started at the age of five to six weeks and

prior to this age, the maternal immunity will be helping the animal to have natural disease resistance. It is always better to deworm the animal before the vaccination and this is given emphasis many times. Vaccination against the parvo virus is done at an early age because pups are often being affected by parvo viral infections. The booster dose for each vaccine needs to be given at appropriate time and this helps to build up the immune status to an appreciable manner. Vaccination is carried out in many countries against rabies disease.

Hence, vaccination against rabies is given more emphasis always. Even rabies tags are fixed on to the dog collar of most of the dogs. Rabies vaccine is given at age of thirteen to fifteenth weeks of age and is repeated in fifteenth months time. However, this depends on the type of vaccine used. Once in three years, this is repeated.

In dogs that have not received colostrums or dogs at high risk areas, give measles virus vaccine and killed parvovirus vaccine before five weeks of age itself. Leptospira serovar vaccine is given at six to eight weeks of age and again at tenth to twelfth weeks and at thirteenth to sixteenth weeks.

Then annually repeat this. Bordetella and lyme disease vaccinations are only optional ones in case of dogs. Vaccinations against the canine parainfluenza, canine parvovirus, and canine adenovirus type- two is similar to the schedule maintained with leptospiral serovars.

27. Common questions about vaccinations

Common questions about vaccinations are to be understood by the dog owners, as a priority. One of the common questions is whether the dog needs to be given vaccination on the first week of age or not. The dogs need not be vaccinated within five to six weeks of age. But, if they did not receive vaccinations, then the vaccination against the parvoviral infections used to kill viral vaccines and measles disease may be given.

Another common question is whether dog is to be given bordetella disease vaccine and lyme disease vaccine. No, these vaccines are only optional. Can the parvoviral vaccine can be used in first week of life? No. This will interfere with maternal antibody levels.

Can a pregnant animal be vaccinated? Yes. Two to three weeks earlier to pregnancy activity that is expected, the pregnant animal may be vaccinated against viral diseases. This helps to provide maternal antibodies to the young one to be given birth. Is there any need to give rabies vaccine to dogs? Yes. It is a must to go for the anti rabies vaccine for dogs.

When this anti-rabies vaccine is given to the dogs, what precaution does one need to undertake in this regard? Rabies vaccine is given at age of thirteen to fifteen weeks of age and should to be repeated in fifteen months and then once in three years. It is important that the dog is given this vaccine.

However, this depends on the risk area. Is there any need for canine distemper vaccination in case of dogs? Yes. There is a specific requirement in the case of dogs for the vaccination against the canine distemper. This disease is more prevalent in most of the countries.

Is there any vaccination against leptospirosis and at what age, the dog is to be vaccinated? This is to be given at age of at six to eight weeks of age, again at tenth to twelfth weeks, and again at thirteenth to sixteenth weeks of age.

28. Spaying and neutering

Spaying and neutering of dogs are highly wanted if you don't want to breed the dogs and however, these activities need to be carried out by qualified veterinarians specialized in pet care and management. Anesthesia is required along with due surgical procedures for carrying out the spaying and neutering.

One has to understand first the terms like spaying or neutering. Both are related to the surgical approaches of sterilization in case of females and males respectively. However, the term neutering is also related to such procedures in both sexes. Accidental pregnancies that are not wanted can be highly minimized by these procedures.

Spaying and neutering helps to prevent occurrence of pyometra, which is a common reproductive disorder-giving problem to the dog owners. In male dogs, the neutering helps to prevent the occurrence of prostate enlargement or cancer. Hence, these help to minimize the incidences of reproductive disorders in dogs.

By these spaying and neutering, the male dog's desire in search of female dog in heat is highly minimized and hence, wandering of male dog is reduced. The animal becomes calm also by these surgical remedies. Territorial behavior of these animals is also highly minimized by these in case of male dogs.

Spaying of your dog before the occurrence of first heat is the best one to avoid the incidence of breast cancer. If the dog is spayed after the first heat, the chances of occurrence of breast cancer in them is more and has been proved by research. Younger group of dogs need to be subjected to these operations to avoid complications in future.

Many veterinarians prefer the spaying and neutering of dogs only at the age of five to six years. However, these can be performed even at the age of three to five years. Postoperative care needs to be followed meticulously to avoid the occurrence of infections by microbial organisms.

29. Spaying of the Female dog

Spaying of the female dog is undertaken to control the unwanted pregnancy by crossing of some unknown or country or non-descript dogs. The spaying of the dog reduces the aggressiveness of the dog. By spaying, one can reduce the incidences of the commonly encountered reproductive diseases like pyometra.

Spaying also helps to control the population in case of stray animals and many nations are doing these operations by removing the ovaries from the female animals. Experienced veterinarians are required to do the spaying in case of female dogs and the postoperative care is to be given more emphasis. If proper control measures are not taken after the surgical operation for the removal of ovary, then the infections may start setting in and the animal may end up in development of peritonitis and then toxemia sets in, causing unwanted health problems.

Death of the dog may finally occur, if the dog is not provided an effective and proper veterinary care. A female dog that is spayed before the occurrence of first heat will have almost a zero chance of development of mammary cancer, which is more common with the dogs that are not spayed.

A female dog generally comes to heat once in eight months or so. During the heat occurrence, there is bleeding from vagina and the dog may cross with the unwanted male and the spaying activity prevents all these. In case of aged dogs, the dog may often get signs of increased thirst, anorexia, vomiting etc. that are so common with pyometra.

Pyometra means the presence of pus in the uterus. Once pyometra occurs, it involves many discomforts to the animal in addition to the cost factor involved for the therapy also. Such pyometra is totally prevented by spaying because in the case of spaying, you are removing both ovaries and the uterus.

30. Surgical neutering of the male dog

Surgical neutering of the male dog is important in helping the dog owners to control the male dog's aggressive behavior. Yes. By doing the surgical neutering, it becomes possible to control the dog's restlessness, which might have caused so much agony for the owner and hence, neutering corrects such activity to the benefit of the dog owner.

When the dog is in puppy stage, the dog may be subjected to the surgical neutering technique. Hence, the hormonal impact is highly minimized in such male dogs.

The surgical neutering of the male dog helps to prevent the incidences of prostate gland diseases. Generally, in case of male dogs, the prostate enlargement is more common. In canine patients undergone the surgical neutering, the incidences of such prostate enlargement are totally minimized.

Sometimes, the adult male dog has more difficulties during defecation. However, one has to rule out the feed borne constipation like lack of fibers etc. before resorting to the fixation of prostate enlargement as a cause for this. Constipation is mainly due to the increased size of the prostate gland. Neutering makes shrinkage of the prostate gland. In surgical neutering, the incision is placed in front of the scrotum and the testicles are removed in a surgical manner using aseptic techniques.

The wound need not be closed except the tying up of the cord after cutting of the testicle. However, in two to three days time, as a routine tissue reaction, some swelling may occur in the scrotum. However, once you administer the antibiotic that has a broader spectrum of activities, the condition gets recovered in a satisfactory condition. Septic shock may occur if the surgical site gets infected with some microbial infections and in these cases, the wound needs a thorough dressing procedure and the patient needs to be continuously monitored in a clinical environment.

Take note that local animal organizations perform the surgical neutering when the stray male dogs are captured by them.

31. Pet health insurance

Pet health insurance is highly required nowadays because of the escalating cost factors pertaining to the health maintenance in dogs and other animals. Dog owners need to find pet insurance firms that settle dues to the pet owners without much delay and in a more appropriate manner. Pet health insurance firms recently come forward to settle the dues in a proper manner after the due verification of the claim. If anything happens, dog care costs can add up without insurance.

Hence, know the approved list of your local animal care hospitals. Even have the list of veterinary experts who are specialized in dog's health care and disease management measures. Many firms cover up the cost made towards undertaking of surgeries, radiographic examinations, treatment of specific conditions, laboratory fees towards undertaking of various laboratory examinations, and more. There is a weighting period before the approval of your policy by most of the insurance firms after the enrolling from you so it's good to start early.

If you don't like the insurance firm, at any time, you can cancel the insurance policy. A licensed veterinarian list should be available with all insurance firms. Many payment options are available for the pet owners.

It is better to enroll the dogs or other pets before they become adults. The animals when they are young need to be enrolled as a priority.
It is always better to the consumers who are the dog owners. Before the dogs have any illness, accidents, or get into the pre-existing conditions as quoted by many pet health insurance firms, insurance coverage needs to be entered by the dog owners. The medical history of your dog will be subjected to the full review by the insurance firms, so start soon.

32. Clipping a dog

Many dog owners generally think of clipping as only a mechanical activity. Few understand that clipping a dog is an art. Clipping a coat or nail needs to be carried out in a careful manner to avoid the injuries to the skin or nail. Clipping of the coat is to be taken care of as per the breed characteristics. If the coat is not properly clipped, this may lead to the dust accumulation in the coat and the animal may start showing signs of skin diseases. This is true especially when the grooming activities are not done in a proper manner.

Clipping of coat helps to get rid of the parasitic burden to a greater extent and also, the clipping of your dog is of more useful to expose on the type of parasitic problem that the dog is likely to suffer. Many pet health parlors are available wherein the clipping of dog will be carried out in a more systematic manner.

Always make use of a sharp clipper and in the winter regions, avoid the close clipping. This is due to the fact that the closer clipping in the winter seasons may expose the dog to the environmental stresses like the cold climate. Hence, the dog may become more vulnerable to the frostbite. Avoid the close clipping of coat or nail because this may cause injury to the underlying tissues and may cause bleeding in the concerned animal.

Many pet owners need to avoid any clipping activity when the animal is not in healthy status. Clipping instruments are available to a greater extent in many pet shops. Avoid the blunt instruments because they may not clip well and hence, repetition is required often. Always use modern equipments for clipping activities.

33. First steps in grooming

Grooming is one of the important activities to be known well by the dog owner. If the dog owner is not aware of the grooming, then the dog may encounter many types of diseases. First steps of grooming consists of activities like maintenance of coat, nails and ears. The maintenance of the coat mainly consists of enrichment measures like proper bathing, combing, drying of skin by dryers, and more. The animal need not be bathed daily and this helps to protect the skin's characteristics like insulation feature.

Use conditioners and shampoos that are meant for dogs. Combing needs to be carried out with a soft brush meant for use in case of dogs. There are varieties of brushes available and depending on the type of breeds, one can use the concerned brush. This grooming of the coat by a comb needs to be carried out daily and the fallen hair if any needs to be placed in dust bin always.

Otherwise, when the dog owners switch on the fan, the hair will fly and may enter the nostrils of persons. Always don't clip too much because this may lead to injuries of nail always. Similarly, you need to carry all the materials required for the clipping with you before the start of the procedure.

Use a sharp clipper designed for use in case of dogs. It is better to have the dog on the raised place and hence, the control of the animal is easier. Ear canals are to be checked up frequently and sterile cotton may be used for cleaning purposes. Grooming associated guidelines need to be followed strictly by the dog owners.

Nail-maintenance is one of the first steps of grooming activities. Live nail areas can be easily clipped away and are always light colored than the reddish area of the nail in the higher position. During the holding of your dog's feet by you, always have a firm grip. If not, the dog will take an upper hand during the clipping and some injury may occur.

34. Bathing a dog

Bathing a dog needs to be given more emphasis. This is because of the fact that if you are careless in bathing, the animal may end up having some infections. For example, if you don't close the ears with large cotton ball, the water may enter into ear canals and may cause some ear infections with signs like constant discharge from the ears and shaking of head.

Frequency of bathing actually depends on the breed of the dog. If the dog is of a hairy type like the cocker spaniel, then the bathing is to be carried out once in six to eight weeks. If these breeds are bathed too frequently, then the skin and coat loose the protective characters. However, when the dog has defecated on the skin due to the frequent digestive upsets leading to diarrhea, to avoid the bad smell, the dog may be subjected to frequent bathing some times by the owners.

Take more care in avoiding some irritant soaps or human soaps. The soap materials used for human beings are not suitable for dogs. Similarly, many human shampoo products are having some ingredients that are not suitable in the proportions that are to be used in case of dogs. Hence, always try to use the shampoo products that are mentioned mainly for use in dogs. Take more care in using any new product.

Always have good time and patience for products required for bathing in one place with availability of water source. Dogs love the sprinkling of water, river, and oceans. Even when you are using bathtub, have everything in one place and then start bathing of the dog. Try to have a leash, conditioner, towel, and shampoo in the bath place.

Conditioner is of helpful to make the combing activity easier later. Bathing should be a convenient activity to both the dog and the owner. This should not be a burden.

35. Pet Identification

Pet identification is highly required in these days because of the need for the licensing of the dog in a proper manner and to reduce the numbers of the stray dog menace in streets. Pet identification is done by many methods, which are different from each other. The cost factor for that also has variations accordingly.

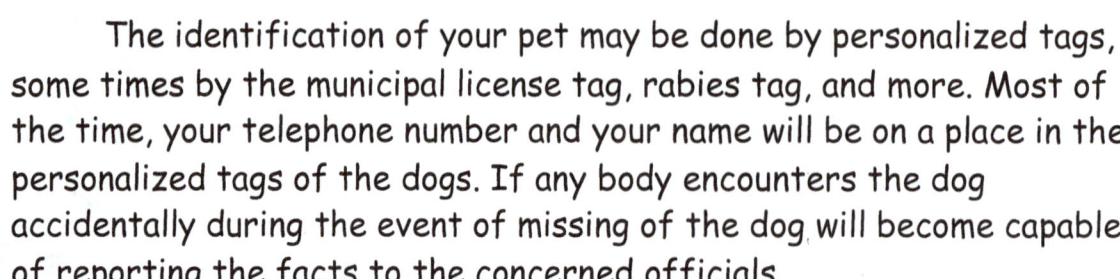

The identification of your pet may be done by personalized tags, some times by the municipal license tag, rabies tag, and more. Most of the time, your telephone number and your name will be on a place in the personalized tags of the dogs. If any body encounters the dog accidentally during the event of missing of the dog will become capable of reporting the facts to the concerned officials.

Plastic and metal pet identification tags are available in multiple colors and the dog owners can choose the color they want. However, many select the reflective type of dog tags along with the collars. Hence, the dogs can be identified even in darkness to a greater extent.

Nowadays, many electronic gadgets are available like microchips which are embedded into the dog. However, these kinds of electronic chips need to be implanted behind the ears and once implanted, this will reveal all the data embedded in this in the computer. A collard and tagged animal makes an indication that it is not a stray animal and this gives more security to the dog.

Traditional forms of identification of the animal like tattooing is now a day not carried in dogs. Thus tracing the missed animal will become easier for the pet owners mainly due to the identification-based dog collars.

Dog Owners Guide

Owning and training your dog

Introduction

Ah, the delightful dog. A furry companion that embodies unconditional love, affection, and loyalty and a charming magnet for attention, too! Picture your future pup frolicking in the sunshine, chasing Frisbees, performing cute tricks, having the occasional mishap at 3 a.m., munching on your prized possessions, and shedding fur across your home. Still eager to welcome a dog into your life? If so, you're in the right spot!

Rearing a dog is like rearing a kid. Some dog owners **PREFER** to rear dogs than kids.

But rearing & caring a dog take up a lot of your time. That is why you got this ebook for more information about rearing a dog for the first time, or just wanted to get more information.

Enjoy this book. Enjoy the journey. Enjoy the times you have with your dog. No wonder people said that "Dogs are man's best friend"

Make sure that you ready to get a dog

Here's the dog-owner's mantra, read it CAREFULLY: *A dog is a living thing. A dog is a living thing. A dog is a living thing*.

Got it? No? Here it goes:

A dog is a living thing.
A dog is a living thing.
A dog is a living thing.

If you want a dog because you think it'll look great in that new BMW you just bought

at 12% interest, think how much fun it will be when it tears up the leather upholstery so thoroughly that even the repo man is impressed. This isn't like buying a new pair of shoes. It's closer to having a child: A child that doesn't speak English and occasionally eats poop. If that thought sends you screaming from the room, consider another kind of pet like maybe a fish or a plant or a pair of shoes.

Repeat the mantra a few more times.

A dog is a living thing.
A dog is a living thing.
A dog is a living thing. If you work from 8 a.m. to 10 p.m. six days a week, you're going to have a lonely,

unhappy dog on your hands. And how do dogs show their unhappiness? In the absence of being able to say, "Pay attention to me, Poindexter," they'll do things like pee on your high school yearbook or methodically eat all your CDs. This isn't their fault.

All together now –

A dog is a living thing.
A dog is a living thing.
A dog is a living thing.

Here's a little "pup quiz" that will help determine if you are ready to add one more member to the family. Answer "yes" or "no" to the following questions:

1. Do you like dogs? I mean do you REALLY LIKE dogs?
2. Does the health of your household allow for a pet dog? (allergies, etc.)
3. Does your building allow dogs?
4. Are you financially secured?
5. Are you OK with picking up dog poop, mopping up dog pee, or cleaning up dog vomit?

If you answered "no" to **anyone** of these, then you're probably not ready to become a dog owner. That's OK though . . . you're still allowed to like them.

Decide on a breed that is suitable for your lifestyle or personality

Getting a pet dog is really a Zenprocess of self-discovery. You can't know the right dog for you until you know yourself. For example, a jock would prefer an active dog. A lazy slug would prefer a dog that doesn't require much exercise. A touchy-feely person would prefer a friendly dog. A tightly-wound person would probably prefer a dog that doesn't bark or shed too much. Think of picking a pup like choosing a mate; you have to find one that compliments your personality.

Here are some very general guidelines. Of course, we won't list every dog breed on the planet, but they'll get you thinking in the right direction:

Poodle

German Shepherd

Keeshond

Intelligent dogs

- Poodle
- German Shepherd
- Australian Sheepdog
- Belgian Sheepdog

Dogs with little exercise

- Dachshund
- Brussels Griffon
- French Bulldog
- Manchester Terrier
- toy breeds (such as a Chihuahua or Pekingese)

Dachshund

Manchester Terrier

Good with kids

- Pug
- English Cocker Spaniel
- Beagle
- Basset Hound
- Brittany Spaniel
- Old English Sheepdog

Pug

Beagle

Good city dogs

- Pug
- Basenji
- Boston Terrier
- Bulldog
- Lhasa Apso
- Welsh Corgi
- Scottish Terrier

Basenji

Scottish Terrier

Quiet dogs

- Basenji
- Borzoi
- Chesapeake Bay Retriever
- Greater Swiss Mountain Dog
- Whippet

Chesapeake
Bay Retriever

Borzoi

Friendly dogs

- Brittany Spaniel
- Bichon Frise
- Old English Sheepdog
- Bearded Collie
- Golden Retriever
- Labrador Retriever

Bichon Frise

Golden
Retriever

There are dozens of breeds and dozensoftraitstosortthemby.Yougettheidea.

Again, these guidelines are EXTREMELYrough.Pickingadogbasedontheselistsis like getting a phone number off a bathroomwall.Therearenoshortcuts.Youcantry going to a dog show or talking to a vet.Inouropinion,though,theabsolutelybest way to research is to **talk to friends whohavedogs**.Believeus;they'llgiveyou more information than you care to know:Sometimesevenmorethanwhatweknow.

In case you didn't realize it, all of the breedswelistedaboveare**purebreds**.This means that they are the product of parentsofthesamebreed.Togetatrue purebred worthy of being in a dog show,youoftenhavetopaythousandsofdollars. Most people get mixes of some sort (the"cockapoo,"acomboofacockerspaniel and a poodle, is quite popular), becauserumorhasitthatpurebreddogscanhave personality problems because the genepoolissosmall(thinkofpeoplewhomarry their cousins). As a result, many peoplechoosetogowitha**mutt**,amish-mashof different breeds. Mutts can combine thebestoftwoormorebreedsinaone-of-a-kind dog. Having a mutt is like the canine equivalent of owning an original work of art. Benji was a mutt. And who doesn't like Benji?

Is this all sounding like too much work? Then go back again to chapter 1 and reread, because the work is just beginning. A dog is a living thing, but **millions of dogs die** every year because their masters didn't realize how much work caring for a dog really is. We're not trying to bum you out, but this is nothing compared to how bummed you'll be if you become one of those failed former dog owners.

Decide what breed is best for your living environment

Now thatyou'vegotyourselffiguredout,it'stimetofigureout what kind of life you lead.

E•v aluate your living space. How much space do you have for a dog? Do you have a fenced yard? What kind of life do you lead? Do you want a great big dog, a little bitty dog or something in between? Sure, that Irish Wolfhound matches your eyes perfectly, but it's not gonna fit into your studio apartment. Conversely, that Chihuahua is never going to be able to navigate your 40-acre spread. It seems obvious, but no matter how well your personality fits a particular breed, you have to make sure that your living arrangements match it too. It would be cruel to keep a big dog locked up all day in a tiny apartment.

E•v aluate your schedule. How much are you home? How many times per day can you walk a dog? If you just thought "*per day*?" then go back to chapter 1 and reread it ten times. Some dogs are more independent than others, so if you're not around a lot, it won't do you much good to get a clingy dog. Always remember that dogs get lonely, and if you're gone for days on end (even if the neighbor pops in just to feed it), the dog'll still get depressed.

A•n ticipate future lifestyle changes. Do you have kids? Will you ever have kids? Are you *sure*? You don't want to get into a situation where you have to put the kid up for adoption because he or she can't get along with the dog. Better to get a kid-friendly dog in the first place, just in case.

Evaluate your activity level. Picture your idea of a fun time, and be sure th• at the right kind of dog fits within it. If you love to go hiking, a Yorkie's not going to be able to keep up. If you like sitting and knitting, a Border Collie's going to make your life a living hell.

Once again, do your homework. Talk to friends, vets, dog breeders, and trainers to find out which breed is best for you.

Make sure you can afford it!

Whoever said that two can live as cheaply as one never had a dog? A dog isn't going to break you financially, but it is an investment. Over the life of the pet, you can expect to shell out as much money as you would on a decent used car (or a crappy new one). But really, which would you rather have - a Yugo or unconditional love? Be honest.

The actual dog isn't expensive (you can get one for **free** at your local animal shelter). Rather, most of the expense will be buying dog food. Ask your vet to recommend a brand.

Vet? What vet? The vet that you're going to take your dog to as soon as you get home from the shelter or breeder, Sherlock. Proper veterinary care is non-negotiable. Things like check-ups, shots, neutering or spaying, flea and tick control, and dental care will keep your dog in good running condition and win you a place in Good Dog Owner Heaven. Once a year is all it takes, assuming your pup isn't playing in the street or smoking a pack a day. But it's still an expense, and you should always have a little backup cash handy in case the dog accidentally swallows your eyelash curler.

Other doggie accoutrements that you'll need to purchase include (for starters):

- Big, sturdy, stable, unbreakable food dish and water dish
- Comfortable, strong collar or harness and matching leash
- Dog bed
- Grooming supplies
- Chew toys
- Current ID tag with address and phone number (really important!)
- Solid, roomy crate for transport (many dogs also use them as a safe sleeping place in the house)
- Warm, dry, wind-and-waterproof doghouse (but your dear little pup will be an indoor dog, we hope)
  Little knitted doggie sweaters are optional in cooler climates.

Pick a place to pick a pup

Breeder

Once you've determined the right breed for your lifestyle, one possibility is to go through a breeder. You can find breeders by looking in the classified ads in your newspaper (the prices are usually pretty steep, ranging from $100 to $3000, depending on the breed and the quality of the puppies). Alternatively, you can call the American Kennel Club at 1900-407-PUPS. The breeder reference person will put you in touch with reputable breeders in your area. Then call several breeders and talk with them; they're a valuable source of information about the breed you've chosen.

Breeders are a good route because you'll get someone who knows all about your breed of dog, so if you have any questions, you'll have a new friend to ask. Also, breeders generally take very good care of their dogs. So good, in fact, that they'll usually interview the prospective buyer to make sure that the dog is going to a loving home. The drawback about using a breeder is the price - you can get a puppy for free at a shelter. But if you're looking for a pretty puppy that you might eventually want to breed or take to dog shows, using a breeder is the way to go.

Animal shelter

Also known as "the pound," shelters are connected with purebred rescue programs, giving you that purebred chic look combined with the warm, gooey, self-righteous satisfaction of rescuing a homeless dog. The benefit of a shelter is that 1) it's free (or really really cheap), and 2) you're saving a dog's life. The main drawback is that the dog could have some kind of personality or health problem (based on how it was treated before you got to the pound). That's a lot to deal with.

As long as you're at the shelter, consider strolling past the puppies and adopting an adult dog. Friendly, well-trained adult dogs will often wind up in the shelter through no fault of their own. Maybe their owner lost the appeal and got sent up the river for 20 to life . . . you never know. Actually, sometimes you *do* know. Many adult dogs come with a written history; some even come with the former owner's contact number so you can get a character reference. Adopt an adult dog and you can save yourself the heartbreak of housebreaking . . . and very probably save the dog's life.

Pet stores . . .

Just say no!

Here's a way **NOT** to get a dog. When you see those little puppies in mall pet stores, our advice is: run away. Many pet stores sell dogs from puppy mills. If you thought that the plight of veal calves was bad . . . well, you're right, it is. But puppy mills are right there with it when it comes to wholesale animal cruelty. They basically churn out puppies for pet stores, kill the ones that don't look like they'd sell well, and keep the live ones in awful living conditions. And pet store puppies that don't get bought are sent to the pound. You can get pet supplies from them, but NOT the puppies please!

Don't be fooled by the breeding papers they'll wave in your face. There's a special place in hell reserved for people who sell puppy mill puppies. It's just down the hall from the place reserved for people who buy puppy mill puppies. You're not rescuing the dog; you're perpetuating the puppy mill industry. Can you tell that we're against this yet?

Prepare yourself for training your dog

Yes, this article is about how to pick the perfect pet dog, but you should also know what you're in for once you get it. If you don't want to get a living hell it is important to train and "fix" your pup, and it's better to get this information sooner than later.

Training

We assume you want a dog because you yearn for the companionship of an animal, not just because you want a new toy (unless it's a toy dog, which, by definition, absolves you). But getting the dog is only part of the equation. To create a wonderful companion and a happy, healthy dog, you have to put some time into obedience training. Just as time on the Stairmaster every day makes for a butt you can be proud of, so too will consistent daily obedience training make for a mutt you can be proud of. At the very least, you'll want to housebreak your pooch. Teaching commands like "sit" and "stay" will make your life a LOT easier. And if you go on to advanced obedience training, you too can have one of those superstar dogs that catches Frisbees and runs obstacle courses when it's not busy signing autographs.

The point: obedience training is how you get the best from your dog. It's also how you give the best to your dog: a well-trained dog is a happy dog. They're secure. They know that you're the boss and that you've got a plan. So keep training in mind when you get a pup.

"Fixing"

Fix my dog? I didn't even know it was broken! But unless you're prepared to take care of 13 more puppies, you really should **spay** (for girl dogs) or **neuter** (for boy dogs) your dog immediately. Millions of dogs die each year in shelters and on the streets, and much of it could be prevented if people had their pets fixed. You might think that having your 'nads snipped off is a bad thing, but the world does not need more puppies. It needs people to take care of the ones that have already been born.

Next to getting married, having kids, buying a house or running a country, caring for a dog is the biggest commitment you'll ever make. You know why: *because a dog is a living thing*. Dogs feel pain, fear, loneliness, joy, love, and loyalty. It's all part of the dog-owning experience.

This ebook has focused almost entirely on the unglamorous responsible side of dog ownership. You already know all the reasons why you want a dog. We wanna make sure you know what you're getting into. But if you take care of your dog properly and treat it with consistent love and affection, you'll be rewarded for your efforts more richly even than people who bought Microsoft at $20 a share. Of course, your reward will be in companionship, not financial security. But who knows? If you train your pup well enough, maybe he'll be sniffing out hot stocks before it's over.

Are you ready to train your dog? If so, move on to the next chapter!

Train your dog

Soyou just got a new dog and want people to see that it can do more than lick itself (and others) in inappropriate places. Or maybe you've finally decided that it's time to show your old dog who's boss - the creature **wearing** *your* **expensive sneakers**, not the one pooping on them.

If you don't have a dog just yet but are planning to get one, keep in mind that while all dogs are trainable, certain dogs are more susceptible to certain types of training. Dobermans are predisposed to be guard dogs, while collies are herding dogs, and setters, pointers, and retrievers are hunting dogs.

Understanding dog behavior

A Tired Dog Is A Good Dog

Give the dog the exercise he needs, and he will spend much of his day resting - not chewing, barking, digging, escaping, or destroying things.

Your Reactions Affect Your Dog's Actions

If you allow your dog to be rewarded for some action, he's likely to repeat it. Consciously allow rewards to happen for actions you like, and prevent your dog from getting rewarded by you or the environment for actions you don't want to encourage.

Dogs Do What Works

Dogs will act in ways that they've learned are successful, ways that gain them Good Things and help them avoid Bad Things. Behavior that is rewarded is going to be repeated.

Be the alpha dog

To successfully train your dog, you must be the leader of your pack, or at least rank above him. **Always be firm and consistent with your dog**, as this will show him that he can't get away with everything, even if he really is the cutest thing alive. If you fear that you may already be underneath your dog in rank, don't concede to defeat and continue to let your dog hog the blankets at night - toss him off the bed. While it may seem mean, it's a good idea to show your dog who's boss by pulling rank on him occasionally. Make him get up from the couch so you could sit in his place, and eat your meal before feeding him his, even if he's drooling a lake by your feet. Don't act scared if your dog growls at you when you ask him to do things - just snarl back without touching him and stand your ground. Continue prodding him to obey you until he does.

Puppies

If you have a puppy, make sure you begin training him as soon as he reaches the appropriate training age; this will reinforce his natural tendency to depend on others. It's also a good idea to start early because in no time at all, your tiny puppy will turn into a monstrous beast with paws the size of your face. You won't want to train "Clifford, the BIG RED DOG"

Older dogs

As for the non-puppy owners, you've probably heard the saying "you can't teach an old dog new tricks." Well, whoever made up that line was either a very successful liar or someone who lacked the patience to really communicate with his/her dog. While it's true that old dogs don't come with clean slates, they *will* obey your foreign commands if you make it worth their while to do so. So don't fall for that fallacy.

Abuse

You should **NEVER** yell at or hit your dog, no matter how frustrating training can get. Going ballistic only teaches your dog to be nervous around you and fear you, making it hard for him to concentrate on what it is you want him to learn. By the way, it's illegal to hit a dog, so if we catch you doing it, we'll throw your butt in jail.

Reinforcement

Reinforcement through repetition and consistency is effective in training *anyone* - Lassie, a feral midget, even you. Habits, good and bad, are formed when an action is repeated over and over again with consistency. So during the process of training your pooch, don't give up the routine until he's got it. And even after your dog has mastered the following tricks, test him on them from time to time to make sure that he's still got it.

Remember Pavel's dog experiment? Though it shows human behavior in the experiment but it also shows a dog's behavior when you reinforce the same concept on a dog. This concept is important when you want to train your dog.

Remember: Repetition with rewardswill reap the right actions/behavior.

Housebreak your dog

The absolutefirstthing your puppy must learn is **housebreaking**: No, no, you don't teach your dog how to break into your house when you forget your keys. Housebreaking means he must learn where and when he may do his business. Besides being substantially advantageous to the hygiene of your household, dogs benefit from having rules and a routine - as pack animals, they look for duties issued by the pack leader and naturally enjoy keeping schedules. Here are the steps to housebreaking your dog:

1. The best age to begin housebreaking your puppy is **between 8 and 12 weeks old**.

2. Experts suggest incorporating a crate in a young dog's training process. (To housebreak an older dog, skip this section.) A crate usually resembles a cage, with a locking door and see-through bars, and should be big enough for the dog to move around in. While it sounds like a miniature jail cell, crates should not be used to punish your puppy. The idea is to make the crate into a doggy bedroom - someplace where your puppy can play and sleep. He should never be confined in his crate for more than two hours at a time.

3. Because dogs, thank goodness, don't believe in eliminating by their sleeping areas, your puppy will not relieve himself in the crate unless you've cruelly locked him in there for longer than he was able to hold it in. Three-month old puppies generally need to eliminate every three hours, so lead your puppy to a designated outdoor bathroom spot often.

4. Try to always leave the house through the same door - the door you'd like your dog to scratch at to signal his need to go out in the future.

5. Try to take your dog out at around the same times each day. A routine will eventually be established, and your dog will soon know to hold it in until you take him out.

6. If your not-yet-housebroken dog is used to roaming freely around the house, look for clues that tell you he needs to go. Your dog may suddenly put his nose down and sniff the ground intently. He may begin to circle an area. Or, he may stare at the door with an intense look on his face. Signs like these tell you to drop what you're doing and get that dog out of the house. If you catch your dog doing his business inside (and **only** if you **catch** him - not after you discover he's already committed the crime), rush over and stop him by grasping his collar, pulling up on it, and saying, "NO" in a deep, stern voice. Then take him outside to let him finish up and praise him with pats on the head or a pleasantly chirped, "Good Fido!" when he does. (Note: Don't say "Fido" if your dog's name is "Rex.")

7. Whenever your dog relieves outdoors, say "hurry up" and then praise him.

   "Hurry up" serves as the trigger words that will eventually make your dog go on command. That's right, if you consistently say "hurry up" as your dog is doing his business, those words will stick in his mind as an indication to let it all loose, and soon he'll be doing just that whenever he hears the command.

Those magical words will make a frigid winter walk much shorter for the future.

8. When issuing commands, use a deep, gruff voice. Even though most of your speech is just garbled psychobabble to your dog, he will notice tone and pitch differences in your voice. So if you normally sound like Angelina Jolie and you suddenly switch to a Tom Cruise intonation to deliver a command, he'll pay specific attention to what you're saying in the authoritative Cruise voice. Conversely, when you're praising your dog, use a high-pitched, happy voice and incorporate his name a lot. Throw in some excited squealing to really get the point across. You may think you sound ridiculous (and you probably do to other humans), but your dog will eat it up. Encouragement is really important, so ALWAYS praise your dog when he does you proud.

9. One final thing on housebreaking your dog - maintain your patience. We know that when the stakes are as high as cleaning dog waste off carpets on an hourly basis and having your entire house smell like a public bathroom, you want him to be housebroken as soon as possible, if not sooner. But losing your temper or giving up on your dog will only set back the rewarding moment when things suddenly click in his head: "I'm being housebroken! Well, why didn't you just say so?"

10. Your dog **WILL have accidents at first**, so don't complain about mopping up dog pee. To stop persistent accidents, just use common sense. If your dog tends to pee during the night, don't give him water before bedtime. If he tends to poop a lot during the night, take him out one last time right before bed, and wake up early to take him again. First cater to his schedule, and then slowly change it to yours.

Teach your dog some basic commands

Around **12 weeks of age**, your dog is ready for some command training.

Pre-training tips:

1. You should hold training sessions with your dog at least twice a day and each session should be approximately 10-15 minutes long (shorter if either you or your dog get impatient or distracted easily).

2. When you first begin training, keep within a quiet, confined location without any distractions, then slowly work your way out to public areas.

3. The first step in training is to figure out what your dog likes so that you can reward him with a desired prize. If your dog is of the food-motivated type, prepare some small treats that don't crumble. The scent of a dirt-size crumb can drive your dog insane and distract him from the task at hand. You want to keep the treats small because you want to be able to give him a lot of them, yet you don't want the training session to be ended by uncontrollable barfing. If your dog loses interest in the treats, switch the type of treat. You may also want to try scheduling training sessions around mealtimes.

4. If your dog is more driven by petting or a chance to play games with you (as many small-sized dogs are), haul out the squeaky ball. Don't get caught up in the petting and playing during a training session, though. Just reward your pooch with less than half a minute of playtime and then get back to work.

5. For the following commands, you'll need your dog to be collared and leashed.

   Collars come in a variety of designs and materials, but a simple nylon one is fine, as long as it isn't slipping off or causing your dog's face to turn blue. If you use a choke chain, make sure it isn't made of chain link, as they can catch accidentally and choke your dog.

Sit

The sit command is possibly the easiest command of them all:

1. Start by facing your dog with treat in hand.

2. **Show** him the treat and as he trots over, **raise** it up and over his head. In a desperate attempt to keep his eyes on the food, your dog will be forced to sit down.

3. **Say**, "SIT" (remember - Connery voice) as soon as your dog starts to do so.

4. Then **reward** him with the treat.

5. If your dog won't sit for the food, **kneel** down next to him, **hold** his collar in one hand, and **push** his rear end gently but firmly down until his rump touches the ground while saying, "SIT." Then **reward** your dog with pats, ecstatic cheering, a party, or whatever else gets your dog's tail thumping.

6. **Repeat** this exercise until your dog sits following the verbal command alone.

7. Always use the same **motion** of raising your hand way over your dog's head while saying "sit." This will teach your dog to also associate the hand movement with the command.

8. Start doing without the treat occasionally (but still the praise) until he no longer needs the treat.

Down

To get your dog to lie down, he must first have mastered the sit command:

1. After telling him to sit, **hold** your dog by his collar, **stick** the treat right in front of his nose, and **move** it downward slowly.

2. Your dog's accursed love of food will leave him no choice but to **follow** the treat down into submission as his restrained collar keeps him from frantically lunging at the treat.

3. **Say**, "DOWN" as he begins his descent and reward him only when he is lying fully on the ground.

4. If your dog's willpower is stronger than his appetite, **kneel** down next to your sitting dog, gently **pick up** his forelegs with both hands and arms, and **lower** him into a lying position while saying, "DOWN." By pulling his forelegs out, he'll be forced to slide down.

5. Then reward him.

6. Start doing without the treat occasionally (but still the praise) until he no longer needs the treat.

Come

This useful command will get your dog to stop doing just about anything and come to you:

1. In the early stages of training, **never** tell your dog to come over to you for an unpleasant reason (he will associate "come" with negativity and be hesitant to do so).

2. Start by **standing** a short distance away from your dog with food or a favorite toy in hand.

3. **Call** out your dog's name and as his eyes zero in on the treat and he starts to walk towards you, **say**, "COME."

4. When your dog reaches you, **respond** by doing a jig in celebration of his sheer genius and giving him a treat.

5. As always, repeat this command until he is willing to come to you even if all you have to offer are your arms and the jig.

During the weeks when you're training your dog to do any of these tricks, if he does an action without your prompting (like if he just happens to walk over to you and sit down), go nuts over his great accomplishment, even though you didn't ask him to do it. Make a big fuss and gush, "GOOD SPARKY! SIT, SIT! *Good boy*!" At first, your bewildering actions will confuse your dog and possibly make him fret over your mental state. But because his major goal in life is to please you, he will soon plant his furry butt on the ground (or whatever it is you want them to do), just to get that wonderfully exciting reaction out of you again.

Any time a training session isn't going well switch to repeating a trick that your dog has already mastered, reward him for following your command properly, and end the session.

Teach your dog some fancy tricks

Let's face it: with commands like "sit"and "come" under your dog's belt, you can take him out in public, but dog food commercial directors aren't pounding down your door. You want a dog that raises eyebrows, attracts comely (human) members of the opposite sex, and pays your bills. While all of these things may not actually happen, we can help you teach your dog a few more fun little tricks.

Shake

1. **Get** your dog to sit first and hold his attention with a treat.

2. Then **pick up** one of his front paws and hold it very loosely in your hand as you say, "SHAKE."

3. **Don't grab** his paw or he'll get freaked out by the pressure and withdraw.

4. **Reward** him immediately and repeat the exercise several times before giving him a chance to place his paw onto your open palm by himself.

5. If he doesn't do it after a couple of seconds, **pick up** his paw for him, while saying, "SHAKE," and guide it into your hand.

6. Eventually, he'll get the idea.

Fetch

You'll need your dog on a long leash or clothesline for this trick:

1. **Catch** his attention with his favorite toy and get him excited by **waving it** around before throwing it a short distance away from you.

2. As he inevitably starts to run towards it, **yell**, "FETCH!"

3. Once your dog picks up the object, don't walk towards him; **wait** until he comes to you.

4. If he starts to wander off elsewhere, **pick up** the leash and gently pull him towards you.

5. **Pet** him on his back and wait for him to drop the toy on his own. (If you try to grab it out of his mouth, he'll interpret it as a tug-of-war game.)

6. If a couple of hours have gone by and you're still waiting for the toy to hit the ground, **present him** with a tasty treat or another toy as an incentive.
7. Then as soon as your dog drops the toy, pick it up and do it all over again.

Door

This is a great trick to teach your dog how to shut doors on his own:

1. **Situate** your dog and yourself in a room where the door closes when pushed towards the doorjamb. (Make sure it isn't a swinging door.)

2. **Position** the door to be only three inches open.

3. **Hold** a treat up against the door, at the height of your dog's nose.

4. **Tell** your dog to come.

5. As he rushes over to claim his reward, **lift** the treat up and away just before he reaches it, so his nose bumps against the door and it gets pushed forward a little.

6. As he comes in contact with the door, **say**, "DOOR," then praise him.

7. **If he doesn't touch the door**, don't reward him; just repeat the exercise until he accidentally does.

8. Have him push the door further and further, until it actually shuts. With consistent practice and patience, he'll soon be slamming doors shut right and left.

If you should come across any specific problems during any of these training exercises, talk to your dog's vet or with other dog owners (the ones with the obedient dogs). Or, check out some dog training discussion forums on-line at www.petopia.com.

Other dog tricks

Thissection covers other dog tricks that you can train when your dog has mastered the basics. Note that PATIENCE is the key to successful dog tricks. Remember Pavel's dog: Repetition with rewards will reap the right actions/behavior.

Most of the actions you see dogs doing in movies are just a bunch of simple tricks. If you learn these tricks, maybe you can be in a movie too. ☺

By teaching your dog to do each trick, you can have him/her capable of being a movie dog (or just a fun pet).

Some of these tricks help the dog in other sports such as agility and in obedience.

Likewise, agility work can be incorporated into movie work. For example, dogs that can jump obstacles can be taught to jump in and out of moving cars, leap over people or other dogs, or jump in and out of windows. A-frame work can be used to teach the dog to go over fences or other high obstacles and dog walk training can be used to teach dog to walk along narrow walls, etc. The circle obstacle with the hole covered with saran wrap can be used to teach the dogs to jump through a window.

This list doesn't include tricks such as retrievals which are used often in movies or bite work. Bite work should only be done by a trained handler as you must do it properly to be effective. None of these tricks require special equipment. They are meant to be fun for you and your dog. This list includes some instructions on how to do them but there are many ways to teach the same trick. Use the one that works for you and your dog.

PLAY DEAD/BANG

Agility Use: to get dog to down on table if you are having problems with this obstacle

How: With dog in sit or stand stay, point finger and pull hand up while saying bang.

This action is similar to the down hand signal. Dog must lie down on side with head down. You may have to do in stages - down and side.

CIRCLE

Agility Use: to improve corners and turns and weaving - helps increase flexibility

How: With dog in stand stay in front of you, give "circle" command and entice dog with food treat or toy to turn in circle. Don't encourage to "chase tail'. Give reward when dog turns fully. Gradually give command from greater distances. For distance, ithelps to put reward on end of pole and use to get dog to turn in circle.

BOW

Agility Use: before doing agility, this is a good stretching exercise. Can also help on down contacts

How: With dog in stand stay, handler in front of dog, with reward (food treat) in hand. Move both hands in towards dogs front paws (above paws) while saying "bow". As dog extends head down for treat in a bow position, reward. This trick is eventually down at a distance and can be down from the side with a single hand command.

CRAWL

Agility Use: Helps dogs who will not go through tunnel

How: Dog in down stay. Hold treat in right hand with left hand on dog's withers (farther back on large dogs). Move hand with treat up and down (short movements) while saying crawl. As dog moves forward, hold him/her down with hand on back. Move treat hand away from dog so dog has to follow to get treat. Reward initially after any movement and then require longer distances. If dog has trouble crawling, this can be down under someone's legs or under a solid chair or low agility table.

BACK UP

Agility Use: positioning dog at start, repositioning if dog slightly overruns weave poles, general control

How: Handler in front of dog. Step into the dog, move hands towards dog in a pushing motion (palms up facing dog). Dog will have to move backwards as you move into it. Reward with "good back" as soon as dog takes one step. Best way to reward is to toss treat into dogs mouth. If you let him take it from your hand it is hard to get distance on this one. Leash can be used to move dog back if he has trouble. Wall keeps dog straight. Gradually stop moving towards dog as you give the verbal command and hand signal. When learned properly, the dog will back away from you in a straight line for extensive distance (depending on comfort zone of your dog).

TOUCH/TARGET

Agility use: use to send your dog to an obstacle or to encourage touching contact

How: Train this one by first having dog touch a piece of paper stuck to the wall. Take dog to wall, command "touch" or "target" and touch the paper. When dog jumps up and touches the paper, reward her. Then place an object on floor and send dog to "touch or target. Reward when dog moves to object and touches it.

TURN OUT LIGHT

Agility Use: same as target - a fun trick to do that helps dog learn to go away from handler and touch or manipulate an object

How: Hold treat at light switch (make sure dog can reach the switch when on back legs. For short dogs, place on sturdy table at light switch). Give command "turn out light" or "light off". When dog jumps up to get treat make sure her paws hit the switch. Reward with "good light off/out", or whatever your command was. Gradually start to stand away from switch and send dog. Toss treat when dog jumps up and paws at light. You can also teach this by placing the treat on the switch so dog has to knock it off. This method may, however cause the dog to use the mouth to hit the switch more than the paw so it is preferable to hold the treat in the hand.

JUMP OVER DOGS

Agility use: Practising jumping obstacles, socializing with other dogs, being handled on obstacles from both sides

How: This is an interesting trick to do once you have a group of dogs that meet certain qualifications:

- Get along (ie non aggressive with each other)
- Keep a still down stay
- Good at jumping low obstacles

If you have this combination, this trick can look very impressive. First start with pairs. Have one dog in a down stay with the handler holding the leash short and a treat in hand if required. The other handler gives the "over" command and while on leash has the dog jump the one who is down. Repeat in opposite direction to get dog used to jumping on both sides of handler. Then switch dogs. When the pairs are reliable, put up to 6 dogs in down stays about 3 feet apart (depending on size of jumper). One dog (on leash to begin) jumps all of the other dogs. This is repeated several times for each dog and then they change places until all dogs have had a turn jumping.

WALK UNDER

Agility Use: apart from teaching a long stretch exercise which is good for warming up, there isn't too much related to agility in this one but its fun and looks good.

How: Same qualifications for dogs as Jumping Dogs. Once all of the dogs can bow and hold it, line up dogs very close together and give the "bow" command at same time. Tell dogs to "stay" - handler holds treat close to keep attention. You need to use a very small dog such as a terrier for the next part. While the larger dogs are in bow position, the small one starts at one end and walks under their rear legs. Trick is to keep the large dogs from lying down. This takes great concentration and muscle control by the large dogs.

SPEAK

Agility use: none

How: This is usually a simple one to teach if your dog likes to bark at you. Trick is to get her to do it on command and from distances. First decide on a hand signal that is not similar to any other. You can use a motion of opening and closing thumb and fingers (facing the dog). Some handlers think this looks more like a mouth opening and closing. Other handlers use a closed fist, twisting motion. Tell your dog to "speak" at the same time. When she does, reward with treat immediately and say "good speak". If your dog doesn't bark readily, continue to give command until she gets really fed up with you and barks. Then quickly reward. She wont know why but if done enough, she'll get the message. Gradually give the command verbally only and then hand signal only. Increase distance to the maximum comfort zone.

WEAVE HEELING

Agility use: improves flexibility

How: Start heeling off leash. Have a treat in both hands. As you step with right foot exaggerate the step and bait dog under your leg while saying "weave". Dog is to walk under your leg to your right side. Then as you take the left foot step, repeat to left side. Continue as you move forward. This trick takes time to learn and if you have a large dog it can be more difficult. The trick is to keep the dog weaving in and out under your legs. Once you have this one, you can combine it with the next trick (circle me) into a complete heeling pattern.

CIRCLE ME

Agility use: circles improve turns and keeps dog focussed on handler. May help in direction changes

How: Start heeling with treat in hand. Bait dog while saying "circle me" and draw the dog around your body so dog is completing a circle around you. Remember to continue to move forward while doing this. Make it lots of fun and get dog to skip around you. This is a fun trick - not an obedience exercise. Change direction until dog can circle you in both directions. When you've got this down to a fine art, do two circle me's, 2 weaves, repeat, repeat. Then make up different combinations. For example: circle me, circle me, weave, weave, circle me, circle me, bow (and then reward). Note that this can takes several weeks to get or your dog may pick it up very fast.

WAVE

Agility use: none

How: Place dog in sit stay. Decide on a hand signal. It can be a circular movement of your hand like a wave or hold hand palm up and wave fingers in and out (as in making a fist). It is not recommended doing a real wave with palm facing down. It looks too much like the speak command and can confuse the dog. Sitting close to your dog give the command and hand signal. If dog doesn't do anything nudge her paw until she lifts it up. Reward. Eventually require her to lift paw higher. Always reward every time she does it. Eventually start to give command from farther back.

HIDE YOUR EYES

Agility use: none

How: The dog can be in a sit or down for this one. The idea is to get her to cover her eyes with one paw on command. It will take some practice to find out the best method for your dog as we find they all respond to different signals. You may prefer to do it in a down. Then with treat in hand, tell the dog to "cover your eyes". Physically lift her paw over her muzzle and reward. If you blow gently on her nose, she may be inclined to swipe at her face. When she does this, reward. You have to just repeat the command and movement until the dog realizes what is needed to get the treat.

BOOK ON HEAD

Agility use: balance

How: Find a book that is suitable to the size of your dog. Balance book either on head between ears, on withers or on muzzle. This depends on your dog's body shape. Hold the dog still with left hand and place book with right. Hold book while saying "stay". Eventually remove both hands (slowly) until dog is balancing book. Count to 3 and remove and release and reward. Idea is to increase time the dog holds the book. The ultimate is to have the dog come while balancing the book. This isa hard one so don't expect instant success.

COOKIE ON NOSE

Agility use: none

How: Hold dogs muzzle and give "stay" or "leave it" command. Place a cookie on top of nose and continue to say "stay" or "eave it". Let go of muzzle. Dog must hold the cookie until you give a release command - "take it". Then she must catch the cookie inher mouth. This is a fun way to give treats and looks cute.

FIND IT

Agility use: none

How: The idea is to have the dog use her nose to find a hidden object. This is good practice for tracking or utility work. First start with simple exercises. Show the dog a treat (strong smelling ones work best). Then let the dog see you place it under the edge of a towel about 6 feet away. Let the dog smell the scent of the treat on your hand. Send dog and say "find it". Reward with praise when she finds the treat. The reward is the treat. Start to move farther back from the hiding place and move the location of the treat - put it further under the towel so it is harder to get out. Then leaving towel in same place, put the treat a few feet away from the towel and send the dog. The dog will have to sniff out the location. Eventually, you will place the dog with her back to the location and have someone make sure she cant see where you put the treat. Then when that level has been achieved, move the dog to another room, hide the treat, let dog sniff your hand and send to "find it". Give lots of praise. You can eventually move from food to solid obstacles such as keys, toys, etc. This makes the exercise into a retrieval.

SNEEZE

Agility use: none

How: The object is to make your dog sneeze on command. The signal will be the handler cupping her hands around her nose and mouth and saying "sneeze". With the handler seated in a chair, have your dog in a sit/stay in front of you. Cup your hands around her muzzle, say sneeze and blow gently into her nostrils. Continue until she either snuffles, sneezes or makes any such motion. Reward "good sneeze" and treat. Repeat. This may take a long time depending on the dog. Some will sneeze immediately, and others will take a lot of work to respond.

GO THAT WAY

Agility use: sending dog to a location

How: The object is to tell the dog to go in a certain direction and she will move wherever you point. First use a bait (can be food or toy). Place three baits - one directly in front of you about 10 feet away, one along the same line (10 feet away) to the right and one to the left. Dog is in sit or stand beside you on long line (or flexi). On command "go that way", point to the treat you want the dog to go to. If dog has trouble, toss a treat in that direction to get her started. Reward when she moves correctly. If the dog goes wrong way, stop her with the long line and direct again. Continue to give the command until there is success. Once dog picks up first treat point to the next one and say "go that way", and so on. The dog must pay attention and move in the direction you are pointing to. Eventually you will start to give commands when the dog is in a position away from you. For example, send your dog to the left (may have to toss a treat.) When she gets there tell her to "down" or "sit". If she does it, walk in and reward. Alternate commands until your dog will obey from longer distances.

SAY PRAYERS

Agility use: none

How: The object is to have your dog put his head down between his paws on the command "say prayers" and to end the exercise on the command"amen". Start with handler seated on a chair, dog in sit/stay in front. Put a treat on chair between your legs. Tell dog to "say prayers" and encourage or lift both front paws on to the chair (NOTE: dog must remain seated). The action is similar to a beg with the paws resting on the chair. Tell dog to "leave it" so he doesn't eat treat and repeat "say prayers". Dog should stick nose down to the treat between paws. Then give release "amen" and reward with the treat. You may find this easier to do on a low table. While standing behind dog, guide paws on to table and encourage him to lower muzzle between paws towards the treat.

Other tips

Here'ssomeother tips in caring and training your dog.

The Crate As A Safe Den

People use crates for lots of reasons, like to help with housetraining or traveling. Our dogs use theirs to sleep in at night. But, the crates are also a great place of escape when a dog's world seems scary. When there is a big thunderstorm, the crate is the perfect size and shape to crawl into and feel protected from the noise and lights. Even a socialized dog that is used to having three or four people come over to visit can be overwhelmed when all the relatives arrive for a holiday - crates come to the rescue.

Crates not only give your dog a place to feel extra safe, they come in handy to actually keep them out of danger. When there are workmen in the backyard, the dogs feel secure in their crates, but they also won't accidentally be allowed to run in the street or get hurt by nails or power tools.

For thousands of years, dogs have had the instinct to den - so providing them with a safe den seems like the least we owners can do. The crate is cleaner than a hole in the ground, and it has the added benefit of being portable and lockable. Dogs are less likely to bark when they can see less, and they feel more protected when "danger" can't see them. What can make a wire crate feel as safe and cozy as a den includes a soft pad to sleep on and a tie-on cover. We prefer the carrier because it is solid (with ventilation holes). With either one, you just need it to be large enough for the dog to be able to change position. A larger one feels less like a safe den and adds the risk of it being used as a bathroom.

Act Like a Dog When Puppy Bites ☺

Puppies bite everything when they are getting new teeth, which helps the teeth come in. But, you do have to stop him from biting people. The best discipline is the kind that his mom would use.

If puppy bites, grab his muzzle with your hand and say no in a mean voice - "in his face." Then leave. Playtime is over.

If puppy doesn't get the message with this, pick him up by the scruff of his neck and shake his body while you tell him no in a mean voice. And, again, playtime is over.

For the really stubborn puppy, put him on his back and hold him down until he calms down and gets the message that you are top dog. If he is little, you can do this in your arms. For the larger puppy, do this on the floor.

Playing tug of war with a puppy encourages him to use his teeth in play. So can wrestling. Instead of these trouble-causing games, you must show him in the beginning that you are top dog. And that goes for everyone in your family. Your family is in danger of future aggression and real biting from a dog that thinks that he is equal to or above any of you.

Emergency Remedy for Swallowed Objects

What do you do if your puppy (or mischievous older dog) gets into your holiday decorations and eats some of the glass ornaments? This potentially lethal mishap can darken even the brightest holiday season.

THE PROCEDURE: BEFORE the holiday go to a pharmacy and buy a box of cotton balls. Be sure that you get COTTON balls...not the cosmetic puffs that are made from man-made fibers. Also, buy a quart of half-and-half coffee cream and put it in the freezer. Should your dog eat glass ornaments. Defrost the half-and-half and pour some in a bowl. Dip cotton balls into the cream and feed them to your dog.

Dogs under 10 lbs should eat 2 balls which you have first torn into smaller pieces. Dogs 10-50 lbs should eat 3-5 balls and larger dogs should eat 5-7. You may feed larger dogs an entire cotton ball at once. Dogs seem to really like these strange treats and eat them readily. As the cotton works its way through the digestive tract it will find all the glass pieces and wrap itself around them. Even the teeniest shards of glass will be caught and wrapped in the cotton fibers and the cotton will protect the intestines from damage by the glass. Your dog's stools will be really weird for a few days and you will have to be careful to check for fresh blood or a tarry appearance to the stool. If either of the latter symptoms appear you should rush your dog to the vet for a checkup but, in most cases, the dogs will be just fine.

Some dogs get pretty scared in the bathtub

They jump around, slip and fall, shiver and shake, and are simply miserable. In the process, you can get even wetter than they do. You spend most of the bathtime pushing and pulling just to keep him from jumping out of the tub and within your reach.

Instead of a bath, give him a shower. This is especially good if you have a hand-held shower head. Your dog should feel much more relaxed and less scared standing on firm ground than in a tub of water. You will probably stay much drier and may even get less of a backache. Your dog can get just as clean and get a more thorough rinse, and the wetting and rinsing process is so much quicker. Dry him off in the shower also so, when he shakes, most of this water will stay inside the shower instead of all over your bathroom.

Feeding your dog table scraps is not always healthy

Some people food is not good for dogs (especially chocolate!), some people food is too fattening, and any amount of people food he eats lessens the amount of dog food he will eat - lessening his intake of the nutrients he needs.

If you run out of dog food, cat food will do in a pinch. And, it contains even more vitamins and minerals than dog food. ☺

Does your dog really have doggy odor? That is, even after a bath? What is causing the strong odor just might be an infection in his ears!

If your dog doesn't like his nails clipped or the trip to the vet to get his

———

shots, do your very best not to call him to you just before these things happen. Instead, just walk over and pick him up (or connect the leash to his collar if he is too large) and go. This way, he won't connect coming to you when you call him with the things he doesn't like - which could stop him from coming to you at all.

By the same token, if you call your dog and he runs through the entire house before coming, don't scold him when he does finally get to you. You don't want him to think he'll get a scolding every time he comes when you call him. In fact, start praising him as soon as he starts to come, which should encourage him instead.

Some dogs have trouble coping when they are left alone.

You'll know if yours does if he was destructive while you were gone or if your neighbors tell you he barked all day. You can teach him to cope, while reassuring him that you will come back - both leading to much better behavior and a much happier dog.

Just like with his first "stay," make the session so short that he is able to succeed. Then, make each session a little longer. He will relate your keys, coat or purse with your long absences, so be sure to take them as you normally would. When your dog is calm and relaxed, leave the room. Give no good-byes, and don't make a fuss. Take your keys and go into the bathroom for two minutes. When you return, ignore him, put the keys down, and go back to your quiet time together. Don't make it a big deal before or after, and he may not either. Also, the time was short enough for him to put together your leaving and returning. Later, make your bathroom stay last about five minutes, and eventually get up to at least ten minutes. Next time, leave the house and stay out for about two minutes. Then, continue these sessions until you are gone longer and longer. After each session, he should feel less panic when you leave, less anxiety while he is alone, and more confidence that you will return. Your coming and going will eventually become just a normal occurrence. It is also helpful to have a few of his toys in the room in case he feels the need to chew on something.

A dog's excess tears can be caused by many things, including blocked tear ducts, abnormal eyelashes, corneal ulcers, a tumor or cyst on the lids or eyes, a foreign object lodged behind the eyelids, dyes in dog food, or dyes in dog bowls.

A wet area on the face, no matter what the underlying cause of the wetness, can be a breeding ground for bacteria and yeast. And, bacterial infections commonly occur at the tear ducts, causing excess tears. Ptirsporum, a red yeast bacteria, is at the root of most yeast infections, and a yeast infection is the most common cause of tear stains. Tear stains also often occur at the same time as a gum infection or ear infection. Staining can also occur on a dog's paws from licking and around his mouth from infected saliva.

You could continually wash away your dog's tear stains, but that affects only the result not the cause. Putting a teaspoon of Natural Apple Cider Vinegar per quart of water in your dog's water bowl can clear up most active yeast infections and prevent future infections. Apple cider vinegar tablets can be used if your dog refuses to drink the treated water. A dog's (and human's) system should be PH balanced (between acid and alkaline), and apple cider vinegar adds the acid that many of us are lacking.

Apple cider vinegar (in its natural form from a health food store, not the pasteurized version from the grocery store) is a natural antibiotic, antiseptic, and deodorant; helps digestion and to remove tooth tartar; prevents tooth decay and hair loss (even mange), prevents and heals gum disease and skin problems; and will discourage fleas.

Puppies are not too smart. After all, they soon think of you as their mother and of themselves as human.

Well, maybe that is smart afterall since both draw you two closer. But, they simply don't know the difference between that great rope with knots that pet stores sell for tug of war and your favorite shoe. This is where you need to show your superior intellect. You need to never, ever let anyone play tug of war with the puppy or you need to teach him to let go on command right from the very beginning. Otherwise, he will dig his teeth into your favorite shoe deeper and deeper as you try to grab it away from him. Tug of war can also cause him to become possessive enough to snap someday when someone tries to take a toy from him.

To get a dog let go of one item simply offer him another, which can be a toy or treat, while you give him a command ("drop it" or "let go" or "out"). Praise him the second he lets the item drop. If you don't pick up the item, you eliminate his desire to guard it. Let him pick it back up, you offer something else while saying the command, and praise him when he lets go.

Learning to let go on command could even save his life someday if he were to pick up something poisonous or sharp. You may even need to have him release his bite on a person someday.

You will know when your dog's digestive system is too alkaline by the yellow spots on your lawn.

A dose of one teaspoon to one tablespoon of apple cider vinegar (depending on the size of the dog) per day will correct the pH imbalance and should solve the problem. The apple cider vinegar can be added to the dog's water or put directly on his food. Two tablespoons of tomato juice on the dog's food twice a day will have the same effect.

Adding apple cider vinegar to your dog's diet has many other health benefits. And, you can use any vinegar to remove skunk odor by rubbing it full strength into his fur. As you may have guessed, tomato juice will also work.

Chasing bicycles can be dangerous for your dog and the cyclist. He starts because it looks like fun. He continues because he wins. So, set him up to lose.

Arrange for a friend to ride past your house while you are outside with your dog. When your dog starts chasing the bicycle, your friend should stop suddenly and yell "No!" as he squirts him in the face with a water gun. If your dog loves water, your friend can use an air horn instead. A third choice is for your friend to drop a sealed can containing lots of coins right in front of the dog. Your dog won't be expecting any of these things, and he won't like any of the sudden "shocks." Most importantly, he loses!

DOG TREATS

Biscuits

Ace'sFavorite Cheesy Dog Biscuits

11/2 cups whole wheat flour11/4 cups gratedcheddar cheese 1/4 pound margarine --
corn oil 1 clove garlic --crushed 1 pinch salt 1/4 cup Milk --or as needed

 Grate the cheese into a bowl and let stand until it reaches room temperature. Cream the
cheese with the softened margarine, garlic, salt and flour. Add enough milk to form into a
ball.
Chill for 1/2 hour. Roll onto floured board. Cut into shapes and bake at 375 degrees for
15 minutes or until slightly brown, and firm. Makes 2 to 3 dozen, depending on size.
Yield: "24 biscuit

Alfie And Archie's Dog Biscuits

* 2 1/2 cups whole wheat flour 1/2 cup dry milk --powder
* 1/2 teaspoon salt
* 1/2 teaspoon garlic powder
* 1 teaspoon brown sugar
* 6 tablespoons beef fat
* 1 egg -- beaten
* 1/2 cup ice water

1. Preheat oven to 350. Lightly oil a cookie sheet. Combine flour, dry milk, salt, garlic

powder and sugar. Cut in meat drippings until mixture resembles corn meal. Mix in egg.
Add enough water so that mixture forms a ball.

Using your fingers, pat out dough onto cookie sheet to half inchthick. Cut with cookie

cutter or knife and remove scraps. Scraps can be formed againand baked.

 2. Bake 25-30 minutes. Remove from tray and cool on rack.

Apple Cinnamon Doggie Biscuits

- 1 package apple, dried
- 1 teaspoon Cinnamon --(I usually just shake some in)
- 1 Tablespoon parsley, freeze-dried
- 1 Tablespoon Garlic Powder
- 1 cup ice water
- 1/2 cup Corn Oil
- 5 cups flour
- 1/2 cup powdered milk
- 2 large eggs
- 1 tablespoon corn oil

Put the apples in a food processor so that pieces are small. Combine in a bowl all of the

ingredients -- can add oil or water if dough is too dry. Using a rolling pin roll out dough to about 3/16" thick (can make thinner or thicker). Using a cookie cutter -- cut into shapes -- place on cookie sheets.

Bake at 350 degrees for approx 20 -25 minutes (until golden).

NOTE: if you substitute corn meal just subtract about 3/4 cupfrom flour and add Corn meal

---

Aunt Bianca's Dog Biscuits

- • 2 1/2 cups whole wheat flour
- Flavoring: Meat drippings, broth or water from canned tuna (enough to make a
  1/2 cup nonfat dry milk powder
  1 teaspoon garlic powder
  1 egg -- beaten

  stiff dough).

Combine flour, powdered milk and garlic powder in a medium sized bowl. Add beaten

egg, flavoring and mix well with hands. Dough should be very stiff. If necessary add more flavoring.
On a well floured surface, roll out dough to 1/4 inch thickness. Cut with shaped cookie cutters of your choice.
Place biscuits on cookie sheets and bake at 350 degrees for 30minutes.

Biscuits For Dogs

- 1 cup oatmeal – uncooked
- 1/3 cup margarine
- 1 tablespoon beef bouillon granules
- 5 1/2 cups hot water
- 1 tablespoon garlic powder -- optional
- 3/4 cup powdered milk
- 3/4 cup cornmeal
- 3 cups whole wheat flour
- 1 whole egg -- beaten

Pour hot water over oatmeal, margarine, and bouillon; let stand for 6 min.

Stir in milk, cornmeal, and egg. Add flour, 1/2 c. at a time; mix well after each addition. Knead 3 - 4 min., adding more flour it necessary to make a very STIFF dough. Roll or pat dough to 1/2" thickness. Cut into dog bone shapes with cookie cutter.

Bake at 325 degrees for 50 min. on baking parchment Allow to cool and dry out until hard.

Store in container.

Boo's Biscuits

- 3 1/2 cup whole wheat flour
- 2 cup Quaker oats
- 1 cup milk
- 1/2 cup hot water
- 2 beef or chicken bouillon cubes
- 1/2 cup meat drippings

Dissolve bouillon cubes in hot water. Add milk and drippings and beat.

In a separate bowl, mix flour and oatmeal. Pour liquid ingredients into dry ingredients and mix well. Press onto an ungreased cookie sheet and cut intoshapes desired. Bake at 300 degrees for 1 hour. Turn off heat and leave in the oven toharden. Refrigerate after baking.

Bow Wow Biscuits

- 2 1/2 cups whole wheat flour
- 1/2 cup wheat germ
- 1/2 cup powdered milk
- 1/2 teaspoon salt
- 1/2 teaspoon garlic powder
- 8 tablespoons bacon grease -- or margarine
- 1 egg -- beaten
- 1 teaspoon brown sugar
- 2 tablespoons beef broth -- or chicken
- 1/2 cup ice water
- 6 slices Bacon -- crumbled, optional
- 1/2 cup cheddar cheese, shredded -- optional

In a big mixing bowl, mix all the ingredients thoroughly to forma dough. Roll the dough out with a rolling pin and use a cookie cutter to make shapes forcookies, Bake cookies at 350 degrees for 20 - 25 min.

Bread Machine Dog Biscuits

- 3/4 cup Beef stock -- *see Note
- 1 egg
- 3 tablespoons oil
- 1 cup all-purpose flour
- 1 cup whole wheat flour
- 1/3 cup Bulgur -- *see Note
- 1/3 cup Bran
- 1/4 cup nonfat dry milk
- 1/4 teaspoon Garlic powder
- 1 1/2 teaspoons yeast

Place ingredients in bread pan according to manufacturers directions and press "Dough" cycle.

When machine beeps, remove dough to lightly floured countertop and with a rolling pin, roll dough out to 1/4" thickness.

Using a dog bone cookie cutter (or any small seasonal cookie cutters), cut out dog biscuits and place on a lightly greased cookie sheet or one sprinkled with cornmeal. Re-roll scraps and repeat till all dough is used up. Place in a warm location and let rise 30 minutes.

Bake at 325 for 30 minutes until brown and no longer soft. Place on a rack to cool. Store in an airtight container.

* Chicken, Vegetable Or use hot water and 2 or 3 -bouillon cubes.

**If you don't have bulgur try substituting something like a 7-grain cereal.

Breath Busters Biscuits

- 1 1/2 cups whole wheat flour
- 1 1/2 cups Bisquick ® baking mix
- 1/2 cup mint leaves -- loosely packed
- 1/4 cup milk
- 4 tablespoons margarine
- 1 egg
- 1 1/2 tablespoons maple syrup -- or corn syrup

Combine all ingredients in food processor, process until well mixed, mint is chopped, and a large ball forms. Press or roll on non-stick surface (floured board or ceramic) to a thickness of 1/4-1/2". Cut into 1x2" strips or with bone-shaped cookie cutter and place on non-stick cookie pan. Bake at 375° for 20 minutes or until lightly browned.

Cool and store in air-tight container.

Makes about 30 medium biscuits.

Buddy Boys Dog Biscuits

- 1 cup whole wheat flour
- 1/2 cup all-purpose flour
- 3/4 cup nonfat dry milk powder
- 1/2 cup oats, rolled (raw) -- quick cooking
- 1/2 cup yellow cornmeal
- 1 teaspoon sugar

Cut in 1/3 cup shortening until mix is coarse crumbs. Stir in 1 egg. Dissolve 1 tablespoon instant chicken or beef bouillon granules in 1/2 cup water. Stir liquid into flour mix with a fork. Form dough into a ball and knead on floured board for 5 minutes. Divide ball in half and roll each portion until 1/2 inch thick. Use a cookie cutter or shape biscuits. Put 6 on a plate and microwave at medium for 5 to 10 minutes or until firm and dry to touch. Turn biscuits over after 1/2 cooking time.

---

heese and Bacon Dog Biscuits

- 3/4 cup Flour
- 1/2 teaspoon Baking Soda
- 1/2 teaspoon Salt
- 2/3 cup Butter
- 2/3 cup Brown Sugar
- 1 Egg
- 1 teaspoon Vanilla extract
- 1 1/2 cups oatmeal
- cup Cheddar Cheese --shredded
- 1/2 cup Wheat Germ
- 1/2 pound Bacon -- or bacon bits

Combine flour, soda and salt; mix well and set aside. Creambutter and sugar, beat in egg and vanilla. Add flour mix mixing well. Stir in oats, cheese,wheat germ and bacon. Drop by rounded tablespoon onto ungreased baking sheets. Bakeat350 for 16 minutes. Cool and let the critters enjoy!

Chicken Flavored Dog Biscuits

- 2 1/2 teaspoons dry yeast
- 1/4 cup warm water
- 1 teaspoon salt --optional
- 1 egg
- 1 cup chicken broth --slightly warmed
- 1 cup whole wheat flour
- 1/2 cup rye flour --optional
- 1/2 cup cornmeal
- 1 cup cracked wheat
- 1 1/2 cups all-purpose flour

In a large bowl, dissolve yeast in warm water. Add salt, one beaten egg, and the warmed chicken broth. Add all flour except the all-purpose flour and mix well. Slowly add all-purpose flour until a stiff dough is formed and it can be kneaded by hand. Knead for only a couple minutes, just enough to get the dough to hold together.

Roll out dough about 1/4" thick and cut with cookie cutters, Place biscuits on a large cookie tray and place directly in a 300 degree oven, they don't need to rise. Bake for 45 min. and then turn off the oven. You can let them sit in the oven overnight and in the morning they will be real hard and good for your dog's teeth.

You could also vary this recipe by adding milk for a milk-bone type biscuit or shortening for a little extra fat. Try different liquids and even honey or molasses, Check with your veterinarian for any other nutritional suggestions.

Dog Biscuits #1

- 2 1/2 cups whole wheat flour
- 1 teaspoon brown sugar
- 1/2 cup powdered milk
- 6 tablespoons butter
- 1/2 teaspoon salt
- 1 egg -- beaten
- 1/2 teaspoon garlic powder
- 1/2 cup ice water

Combine the flour, milk, salt, garlic powder and sugar. Cut in butter until mixture resembles cornmeal. Mix in egg; then add enough ice water to make a ball. Pat dough to 1/2" thick on a lightly oiled cookie sheet. Cut out shapes with a cookie cutter or biscuit cutter and bake on cookie sheet for 25 minutes at 350 degrees. Remove from the oven and cool on a wire rack.
To vary the flavor and texture, at the time the egg is added, add any of the following: 1 c. purred cooked green vegetables or carrots; 6 T. whole wheat or rye kernels; 3 T. liver powder. (The last two items are available in health food stores.)
Butter, margarine, shortening, or meat juices may be used.

Dog Biscuits #2

- 1 envelope dry yeast
- 1 cup rye flour
- 1/4 cup warm water
- 1/2 cup nonfat dry milk 1
- pinch sugar
- 4 teaspoons kelp powder
- 3 1/2 cups all-purpose flour
- 4 cups beef or chicken broth
- 2 cups whole wheat flour
- 2 cups cracked wheat or 1 c. cornmeal

GLAZE:
- 1 large egg
- 2 tablespoons milk

Place2ovenracksintheupperandlowerthirds oftheoven.Preheatovento300 degrees.Sprinklethedryyeast orcrumblethecompressedyeastoverthewater.Addthe pinchofsugarandallowyeasttositina draft-free spot for 10 - 20 minutes.

The mixture should be full of bubbles. If not, theyeastistoooldtobeuseful.Stirwellto dissolvetheyeast.Inalarge bowl, place all the dry ingredientsandstirwelltoblend them.Addthe yeastmixture and3cupsbroth.

Usingyourhands,inthebowl,mixtoformthe dough adding more broth if needed to make the dough smooth and supple. Half a batch at a time, knead the dough briefly on a lightly floured counter. (Keep the secondbatch of dough covered with a moist towel while shaping and cutting the first.)

Rolloutthedoughinto18x13x1/4"rectangle.Cutintodesiredshapesusing31/2"one cutter or 21/2"cookie cutter.Re-rollthe scraps.Repeatprocedurewithremainingdough. For an attractive shine, lightly beat together the egg and the milk.

Brushtheglazeonthecookies.Bake for45-60 min. or until brown and firm. For even baking, rotate the cookie sheets fromtop tobottom3/4ofthewaythruthebakingperiod. Use a small, angled metal spatula to transfer the cookie to wire racks to cool completely beforeusingforthenextbatch.

Dog Biscuits #3

- 3 1/2 cups flour
- 4 teaspoons salt
- 2 cups whole wheat flour
- 1/2 cup dry milk
- 1 cup rye flour
- 1 egg
- 1 cup cornmeal
- 1 package dry yeast (1 T.)
- 2 cups cracked wheat
- 1 pint chicken stock

(Ingredients not generally available at grocery stores may be found at health food stores.)

Dissolve yeast in 1/4 c. warm water. Add chicken stock and pour into dry ingredients. Knead for 3 minutes, working into a stiff dough. Roll dough into a 1/4" thick sheet and cut with cookie cutters (cutters shaped like dog biscuits are available). Bake in 300 degree oven for 45 min., then turn oven off and leave biscuits in oven overnight. In the morning the biscuits will be bone hard.

NOTE: This dough is extremely stiff to work with, but the endproduct is excellent!

Dog Biscuits #4

- 2 3/4 cups whole wheat flour
- 1/2 cup powdered milk 1
- teaspoon salt
- 1/4 teaspoon garlic powder
- 1 egg
- 6 tablespoons vegetable oil
- 8 tablespoons water --(8 to 10)
- 2 jars Babyfood, Meat, Beef, Strained -- *see Note

Mix all ingredients together and knead for 3 min. Roll out to `/1 inch thick. Use a dog bone shaped cookie cutter, and place biscuits on an ungreased baking sheet. Bake in preheated oven at 350 degrees for 20 to 25 min.

MAKES approx. 2 dozen doggie biscuits

Note: Strain. Use beef, chicken or lamb

Dog Biscuits #5

- 1 cup whole wheat flour
- 1 cup white flour
- 1/2 cup powdered milk
- 1/2 cup wheat germ
- 1/2 teaspoon salt
- 6 tablespoons shortening
- 1 egg -- slightly beaten
- 1 teaspoon brown sugar
- 1/2 cup cold water

A special treat for your dog, cutters may be purchased at kitchen specialty stores.

Stir dry ingredients well and then cut in the shortening. Stir egg and brown sugar into the flour mixture. Blend in water. Knead dough 10 to 12 strokes. Flour surface if dough sticks. Roll dough out to approximately 3/8 inches. Cut with a bone shaped cookie cutter. Bake at 325 degrees for 30 minutes or until dough is firm to the touch.

Makes about 40.

Dog Biscuits For Your Favorite Dog

2 cu•ps whole wheat flour
1 cu•p cornmeal
2/3 •cup Brewer's yeast
2 tea•spoons garlic powder
1/2 •teaspoon salt
2 eg•g yolks

3 beef bouillon -- or chicken
1/2 •c up boiling water
Preheat oven to 375 degrees.
Mix well. Working with half the dough at a time, roll dough to 3/8 inch thickness. Cut into desired shapes.
Bake for 20 minutes on ungreased cookie sheet. Turn oven off but leave biscuits in oven until crunchy.
Makes about 1 pound of dog biscuits that you dog is sure to love

Doggie Biscuits

- 3/4 c Hot water or meat juice
- 1/3 c Margarine
- 1/2 c Powdered milk
- 1/2 ts Salt
- 1 Egg, beaten
- 3 c Whole wheat flour

Mix well - roll in to small logs in your hands and bake at 325 degrees for about 50 mins.

Doggy Biscuits

- 1 package dry yeast 1/4 cup warm water
- 2cupsbeef broth-- atroomtemperature
- 1/4 cup milk 1/2cuphoney 1 egg --
- beaten 1/4 cup margarine 1 teaspoon salt
- 21/2cupsflour 1 cup cornmeal
- 1cupwheatgerm 2 cups cracked wheat
- 3/4 cup wheat bran 3/4 cup oatmeal
- 3/4cupgratedcheddarcheese 3 cups
- whole wheat flour
-
-
-
-
-
-
-

TOPPING
- 1 cup beef broth
- 1/2 teaspoon garlic powder
- 3 tablespoons oil

In a smallbowl,dissolveyeastinwarmwater.Inalarge bowl, combine beef broth, milk, honey, egg,bacongreaseormargarine,andsalt.Addyeast/water mixture and mix well. Stir in flour,cornmeal,wheatgerm,crackedwheat,wheat bran, oatmeal, and cheese. Add wholewheatflour,1/2cupatatime,mixingwellafter each addition. Knead in the final amountsofflourbyhandtomakeastiffdough.Continue to knead for 4 to 5 minutes.

Pat or rollto1/2inchthickness.Cutintoboneshapesand place on a greased baking sheet. Coverlightlyandletset(rise)for30minutes

Ellie's Dog Biscuits

* 1 cup bran
* 1 1/2 cups whole meal flour
* 1/2 cup olive oil --sunflower or Soya Olive is great for their coat
* 1/2 cup sunflower seeds
* 1 cup oatmeal
* 1 egg
* 1 cup milk or water
* 1 teaspoon brewers yeast
* 1/2 teaspoon salt or kelp
* 1/2 cup coconut 1
* comfrey leaf -- finely chopped. --(can add parsley etc.)

Mix everything together and form balls (or shapes!) with yourhands.
Place on baking tray and flatten with a fork. Bake slowly at 150degrees C until hard - about 40 - 45 minutes. I double the recipe and it makes heaps-about 2 trays.

Gingham Dog and Cat Biscuits

* 1 cup whole wheat flour 2
* tablespoons wheat germ
* 1/4 cup bran flakes 1/4
* cup soy flour 1 tablespoon
* molasses 2 tablespoons oil
* -- or fat 1 tablespoon kelp
* --or salt 1 teaspoon sage
* 1/2 teaspoon bone meal
* 1/3 cup milk --or water
*

Mix all ingredients together. Knead and shape into crescents,rounds or sticks for dogs.

For cats, roll out and cut into narrow strips or ribbons. Bake25-30 minutes in a moderate oven (350 degrees) until lightly toasted. Watch the narrowstripsas they tend to get done sooner than the others. If the biscuits are not hard enough,leavethem in the oven with the heat turned off for an hour or as long as desired.

Glazed Beagle Biscuits

- 2 teaspoons beef bouillon granules
- 1/3 cup Canola Oil
- 1 cup boiling water
- 2 cups rolled oats
- 3/4 cup cornmeal
- 1/2 cup milk
- 1 cup grated cheese
- 1 egg -- beaten
- 1 cup rye flour
- 2 cups white flour

Add bouillon and oil to boiling water then add oats. Let mixturestand for a few minutes.

Stir in the cornmeal, milk, cheese, and egg. Slowly stir in the flours. Knead on a lightly floured surface until the dough is smooth and no longer sticky.Roll out to about 1/4 inch thick and cut into bone shapes. Place on a greased baking sheet.Spoon topping over biscuits. Turn them over and repeat with other side. Bake at 325for 45 minutes or until lightly browned on bottom. Turn off the oven and leave biscuitsin until cool.

Home Made Dog Biscuits

- 1 package active dry yeast 1 cup warm
- chicken broth 2 tablespoons molasses 1
- 3/4 cups all purpose flour --(1 3/4 to 2) 1
- 1/2 cups whole wheat flour 1 1/2 cups
- cracked wheat 1/2 cup cornmeal 1/2 cup
- non fat dry milk powder 2 teaspoons garlic
- powder 2 teaspoons salt 1 tablespoon milk
- 1 egg -- beaten
-
-
-
-

Dissolve yeast in 1/4 cup warm water, 110 to 115 degrees. Stir in broth and molasses.

Add 1 cup only of the all purpose flour, all the whole wheat flour, cracked wheat, cornmeal, dry milk, garlic salt and mix well. On floured board, knead in remaining flour. Roll out 1/2 at a time to 3/8" thick. Cut in desired shapes. Place on ungreased baking sheet, brush tops with beaten egg and milk mixture. Repeat remaining dough. Bake at 300 degrees for 45 minutes. Turn oven off and let dry overnight.

Makes 42 to 48.

Jake's Dog Biscuits

21/2 cupswhole wheatflour
1/2 cup powdered milk
1/2 teaspoon garlic powder
1/2 teaspoon salt
1 teaspoon brown sugar
6 tablespoons margarine --or shortening
1 egg -- beaten
3 tablespoons liver powder
1/2 cup ice water

Preheat oven to 350 degrees. In a large bowl, combine flour, powdered milk, garlic powder, salt and sugar. Cut in margarine. Mix in egg, then addliver powder. Add ice water until mixture forms a ball. Pat out dough 1/2" thick on alightly oiled cookie sheet. Cut with any size cutter. Remove scrapes and redo. Bake 30 min.

Peanut Butter and Honey Dog Biscuits

3/4cupflour
1egg
1Tablespoon Honey
1teaspoon peanut butter
1/4 cup vegetable shortening
1teaspoon baking soda
1/4 teaspoon salt
1/4 cup rolled oats
1/2 teaspoon vanilla

Heat honey and peanut butter until runny (about 20 secondsinthe microwave. Mix ingredients together and drop by 1/2 teaspoonful onto cookiesheet and bake at 350 degrees Fahrenheit for 8 to 10 minutes. My dog is a Pug, andahalf a biscuit is plenty for her. So if you have a bigger or smaller dog, adjust the biscuitsize (and the cooking time). This normally makes about 45 to 50 biscuits.

Peanut Butter Dog Biscuits

- 2 1/2 Cups Whole Wheat Flour
- 1/2 Cup Powdered Milk --non-fat
- 1 1/2 Teaspoons Sugar
- 1 Teaspoon Salt
- 1 Whole Egg
- 8 Ounces Peanut Butter --(1 jar)
- 1 Tablespoon Garlic Powder
- 1/2 Cup Cold Water

Mix above ingredients together, adding water after other ingredients are mixed. Knead for 3 to 5 minutes. Dough should form a ball. Roll to 1/2 inchthick and cut into doggie bone shapes. Bake on a lightly greased cookie sheet for 30 minutes at 350 degrees.

Pumpkin-Patch Dog Biscuits

- 1 1/2 cups whole wheat flour
- 1 tablespoon brown sugar
- 1/2 teaspoon ground cinnamon
- 1/2 teaspoon ground nutmeg
- 4 tablespoons butter-flavored Crisco
- 1/2 cup pumpkin, canned
- 1 whole egg
- 1/2 cup buttermilk

Preheat oven to 400 degrees. Combine flour, cinnamon and nutmeg and cut in shortening.

Beat egg with milk and pumpkin and combine with flour, mixing well. Stir until soft dough forms. Drop by tablespoons onto ungreased cookie sheetand bake for 12 to 15 minutes. Let cool and serve.

---

raildog Biscuits

- 1 1/2 cups flour
- 1 1/2 cups whole wheat flour
- 1 tsp. garlic powder
- 1 cup rye flour
- 1 egg -- beaten
- 1 cup oats
- 1/2 cup vegetable oil
- 1 cup cornmeal
- 1 3/4 cups beef broth --or chicken
- 1/4 cup liver powder -- available in health food stores

Preheat oven to 300F. Mix all dry ingredients in a large bowl.Add egg, oil, and beef broth. Mix the dough, adding enough additional flour to makeadough that can be rolled. On a floured surface, roll to 1/2" thickness, then cut into shapesor squares. Prick with a fork. Bake for 2 hours. Turn the oven off, and let biscuits standin oven overnight to harden. Store in airtight container.

Vegetarian Dog Biscuits

- 2 1/2 cups flour
- 3/4 cup Powdered Milk
- 1/2 cup vegetable oil
- 2 tbs. brown sugar
- 3/4 cup Vegetable Broth
- 1/2 cup carrots --optional 1 egg

Preheat oven to 300F. Mix all ingredients into a ball and rollout to about 1/4" thick. Cut with bone-shaped cookie cutter, or strips, or a cutter shape ofyour own choice. Place on ungreased cookie sheet and bake 30 minutes at 300F.

Western Ranch Biscuits

- 1 package dry yeast 1/4 cup warm water 2
- cups beef broth -- warm 1/4 cup milk 1/2
- cup honey 1 egg -- beaten 1/4 cup bacon
- grease -- or margarine 1 teaspoon salt 2
- 1/2 cups flour --(white, oat, or rye) 1 cup
- cornmeal 1 cup wheat germ 2 cups
- cracked wheat 3/4 cup wheat bran 3/4 cup
- oatmeal 3/4 cup grated cheddar cheese 3
- cups whole wheat flour -- (approximately)
-
-
-
-
-
-
-

Topping:
- 1 cup beef broth
- 1/2teaspoongarlicpowder
- 3 tablespoons oil

Inasmallbowl,dissolveyeast in warm water. In a large bowl,combine beef broth, milk, honey,egg,bacongreaseormargarine, and salt. Add yeast/watermixture and mix well. Stirinflour,cornmeal,wheat germ, cracked wheat, wheat bran,oatmeal, and cheese. Addwholewheatflour,1/2cup at a time, mixing well after eachaddition. Knead in the finalamountsofflourbyhand to make a stiff dough. Continuetoknead for 4 to 5 minutes.Patorrollto1/2inch thickness. Cut into bone shapesandplace on a greased bakingsheet.Coverlightlyand let set (rise) for 30 minutes.Bakeina 350û oven for 45 minutesoruntillightlybrowned on bottom. Prepare toppingduringlast few minutes. Turnoffovenheat.Removebiscuits from oven. Immediatelydipbiscuits in topping. Returnthemtoovenandleave biscuits in oven for several hoursorovernight.

Wheatless Tuna Biscuits

- 1 cup yellow cornmeal -- *see Note
- 1 cup oatmeal
- 1/4 tsp. baking powder
- 1/2 tsp. garlic powder
- 1 small can tuna in oil -- undrained
- 1/3 cup water

Grind oatmeal in processor to make a coarse flour. Set aside in small bowl. In food processor, whirr tuna with the oil, and water then add all the rest of ingredient. Pulse till mixture forms a ball, Pulse to knead for 2-3 minutes. Knead on floured surface till it forms a soft ball of dough. Roll out to a 1/8"-1/4" thickness. Cut into shapes. Bake on lightly greased cookie sheet , at 350 for 20-25 minutes. Cool completely.

Note: or 1/14 cup corn flour

Wholesome Whole-Wheat Biscuits

- 2 1/2 cups whole-wheat flour
- 1/2 cup self-rising flour
- 1 tablespoon beef bouillon packet
- 3 tablespoons powdered milk -- optional
- 2 cloves garlic --crushed
- 1 whole egg --beaten
- 1 tablespoon molasses
- 3 tablespoons canola oil
- 1/4 cup water
- 2 tablespoons water

Measure dry ingredients into bowl. Blend with all other ingredients and chill for one hour.
On a floured surface, roll dough to 1/8 inch thickness and cut with cookie cutters or into strips 1 x 3 inches.
Bake at 300 degrees on cookie sheets for 30 minutes. Brush with melted butter if desired. Cool and serve.

Wolf-Dog Biscuits

- 2 cups whole wheat flour
- 3/4 cup cornmeal
- 4 tablespoons vegetable oil
- 2 cups all-purpose flour
- 4 beef bouillon cubes
- 2 cups boiling water
- 10 tablespoons bacon bits --optional garlic

Combine first 4 ingredients; mix well. Dissolve bouillon cubes in

boiling water and add bouillon to flour mixture. Mix to make stiff dough. Roll onto a floured surface. Cut out shapes with cookie cutters (or a drinking glass turned upside down can be used). Bake in preheated 300 degree
oven for 30 minutes. Let stand overnight to harden.

This is the basic recipe.

Variations could be that you use clear gravies from turkey, roast beef, etc. In place of bouillon cubes or clear soups. Crisp sausage bits could be used in place of bacon. Different spices could also be used (Italian, parsley,
thyme, etc.).

Treats
AnApple a Day Dog Treat

- 2cups whole wheat flour
- 1/2 cup unbleached flour
- 1/2 cup cornmeal
- 1 apple -- chopped or grated
- 1 egg -- beaten
- 1/3 cup vegetable oil
- 1 tablespoon brown sugar, packed
- 3/8 cup water

Preheat oven to 350 degrees. Spray cookie sheet with vegetable oil spray. Lightly dust work surface with flour. Blend flours and cornmeal m large mixing bowl. Add apple, egg, oil, brown sugar and water; mix until well blended.
On floured surface, roll dough out to 7/8-inch thickness. Cut with cookie cutters of desired shape and size. Place treats on prepared sheet.
Bake in preheated oven 35 to 40 minutes. Turn off oven. Leave door closed 1 hour to crisp treats. Remove treats from oven.
Store baked treats in airtight container or plastic bag and place in refrigerator or freezer.
MAKES 2 to 2 1/2 dozen

Apple Crunch Pupcakes

- 2 3/4 cups water
- 1/4 cup unsweetened applesauce
- 2 tablespoons honey
- 1 medium egg
- 1/8 teaspoon vanilla extract
- 4 cups whole wheat flour
- 1 cup apple, dried
- 1 tablespoon baking powder

Preheat oven to 350 degrees. In a small bowl, mix together water, applesauce, honey,

egg, and vanilla. In a large bowl, combine flour, apple chips, and baking powder. Add liquid ingredients to dry ingredients and mix until very well blended. Pour into greased muffin pans, Bake 1 1/4 hours, or until a toothpick inserted in the center comes out dry. Store in a sealed container.

Makes 12 to 14 pupcakes

Baby Food Doggie Cookies

- 3 jars baby food, meat, beef, strained -- *see Note
- 1/4 cup cream of wheat --*see Note
- 1/4 cup dry milk

Combine ingredients in bowl and mix well. Roll into small balls and place on well-greased cookie sheet. Flatten slightly with a fork. Bake in preheated 350 degree oven for 15 min. until brown.

Cool on wire racks and STORE IN REFRIGERATOR. Also freezes well.

NOTE: Carrot, Chicken or Beef baby food. substituting wheatgerm for cream of wheat.

Birthday Cake for Pups

- 1 1/2 cups all-purpose flour
- 1 1/2 teaspoons baking powder
- 1/2 cup soft butter
- 1/2 cup corn oil
- 1 jar baby food, meat, beef, strained
- 4 eggs
- 2 strips beef jerky -- (2 to 3)

Preheat oven to 325 degrees. Grease and flour an 8x5x3 inch loaf pan. Cream butter until smooth. Add corn oil, baby food, and eggs. Mix until smooth.

Mix dry ingredients into beef mixture until batter is smooth. Crumble beef jerky and fold into batter. Pour batter into loaf pan. Bake 1 hour and 10 minutes. cool on wire rack 15 minutes. Ice with plain yogurt or cottage cheese.

Store uneaten cake in refrigerator.

BJ'S Peanutty Pupcicles

- 1 ripe banana
- 1/2 cup peanut butter
- 1/4 cup wheat germ
- 1/4 cup chopped peanuts

Mash banana's and peanut butter, stir in wheat germ. Chill 1 hour. Place in container, store in refrigerator or freezer.

Bone A Fidos

- 2 1/4 teaspoons Dry yeast
- 1/4 cup warm water -- (liquid measure)
- 1 Pinch sugar
- 3 1/2 cups All-purpose flour
- 2 cups Whole wheat flour
- 2 cups Cracked wheat
- 1 cup Rye flour
- 1/2 cup Nonfat dry milk
- 4 teaspoons Kelp powder
- 4 cups Beef broth -- or chicken

GLAZE:
- 1 large egg
- 2 tablespoons Milk

Equipment: Cookie sheets lined with parchment or aluminum foil; rolling pin; 3-31/2" bone cutter or 2 1/2" round cookie cutter.

Place 2 oven racks in the upper and lower thirds of the oven. Preheat oven to 300 degrees.

Sprinkle the dry yeast or crumple the compressed yeast over the water (110 degrees if dry yeast, 100 degrees if compressed yeast). Add a pinch of sugar and allow the yeast to sit in a draft-free spot for 10 - 20 minutes. The mixture should be full of bubbles. If not, the yeast is too old to be useful.

In a large bowl, place all the dry ingredients and stir to blend them. Add the yeast mixture and 3 cups of the broth. Using your hands, in the bowl, mix to form the dough, adding more broth if needed to make the dough smooth and supple. Half a batch at a time, knead the dough briefly on a lightly floured counter. (Keep the second batch of dough covered with a moist towel while shaping and cutting the fast.)

Roll out the dough into an 18 x 13 x 1/4" rectangle. Cut it into desired shapes, using a 3 - 3 1/2-inch bone cutter or a 2 1/2-inch round cookie cutter. Re-roll the scraps. Repeat the procedure with the remaining dough.

For an attractive shine, lightly beat together the egg and milk. Brush the glaze on the cookies. Bake for 45 to 60 minutes or until brown and firm.

For even baking rotate the cookie sheets from top to bottom three quarters of the way through the baking period. Use a small, angled metal spatula or pancake turner to transfer the cookies to wire racks to cool completely.

Store in an airtight container at room temperature. The dough must be used immediately. The baked cookies will keep for many months.
Allow cookie sheets to cool completely between batches.

Bone Bonanza

- 1/2 pound ground beef -- uncooked
- 1/4 cup chicken broth
- 1/3 cup black beans, cooked -- mashed
- 1/3 cup cottage cheese
- 1 teaspoon soy sauce

Combine ground meat and chicken broth in a bowl. Add the black beans and cottage cheese. Add soy sauce. Mix all of the ingredients together thoroughly. Mold the mixture into bone shapes and place on a cookie sheet. Bake for 45 minutes in a 375 degree oven. Let cool.

Bulldog Banana Bites

- 2 1/4 cups whole wheat flour
- 1/2 cup powdered milk -- nonfat
- 1 egg
- 1/3 cup banana -- ripe, mashed
- 1/4 cup vegetable oil
- 1 beef bouillon cube
- 1/2 cup water -- hot
- 1 tablespoon brown sugar

Mix all ingredients until will blended. Knead for 2 minutesonafloured surface. Roll to 1/4 " thickness. Use a 2 1/2" bone shaped cookie cutter (oranyone you prefer). Bake for 30 minutes in a 300 degrees oven on ungreased cookie pans.

Bulldog Brownies

- 1/2 cup shortening
- 3 tablespoons honey
- 4 eggs
- 1 teaspoon vanilla
- 1 cup whole wheat flour
- 1/4 cup carob flour
- 1/2 teaspoon baking powder

Frosting
- 12 ounces nonfat cream cheese
- 2 teaspoons honey

Cream shortening and honey together thoroughly. Add remaining ingredients. Beat well. Bake in a greased cookie sheet (10x15") for 25 minutes at 350 degrees. Cool completely.

FROSTING: Blend together. Spread frosting over cool brownies. Cut into 3 inch or 1 1/2 inch squares.

Canine Carrot Cookies

- 2 cups carrots -- boiled and pureed 2 eggs 2 tablespoons garlic --
- minced 2 cups unbleached flour -- *see Note 1 cup rolled oats 1/4
- cup wheat germ *or rice flourorrye flour.
-

Combine carrots, eggs and garlic. Mix until smooth. Adddryingredients. Roll out on heavily floured surface and cut into bars or desired shapes.Bake at 300 degrees for 45 minutes or to desired crunchiness. The centers will continuetoharden as they cool. Brush with egg white before baking for a glossy finish.

Canine Cookies #1

- 1 1/2 cups whole wheat flour
- 1 cup all-purpose flour
- 1 cup powdered milk -- non-fat
- 1/3 cup bacon grease --*see Note
- 1 egg -- lightly beaten
- 1 cup cold water

In a bowl, combine flour and milk powder. Drizzle with melted fat. Add egg and water; mix well. Gather dough into a ball. On floured surface, pat out dough. Roll out to 1/2 inch thickness. Cut into desired shapes. Gather up scraps of dough and repeat rolling and cutting. Bake on ungreased baking sheets in 350 degree oven for 50 - 60 minutes or until crispy.

Note: Beef fat or Chicken fat can be used

Makes about 36 - 2 1/2 inch biscuits. Store in the fridge.

Canine Cookies #2

- 1/2 cup nonfat dry milk
- 1 egg -- well beaten
- 1 1/4 cups all-purpose flour
- 1 1/4 cups wheat flour
- 1/2 teaspoon garlic powder
- 1/2 teaspoon onion salt
- 1 1/2 teaspoons brown sugar
- 1/2 cup water
- 6 tablespoons gravy
- 2 jars baby food, meat, beef, strained

Combine ingredients and shape into ball. Roll out on floured board, Use extra flour if needed. Cut with knife or cookie cutter. Bake at 350 degrees for25 to 30 min. Cool. Should be quite hard.

Canine Cookies #3

- 1/2 cup dry milk
- 1 1/2 teaspoons brown sugar
- 1 egg -- well beaten
- 1/2 cup water
- 2 1/2 cups flour
- 6 tablespoons gravy
- 1/2 teaspoon garlic salt
- 1 jar baby food, meat, beef, strained -- or more if needed

Combine and shape into ball and roll on floured board. Use extra flour if needed. Cut to desired shape, Bake at 350 degrees for 25 -30 min. Cool. Should be hard.

Champion Cheese & Veggies Chews

- 1/2 cup grated cheese --room temp.
- 3 tablespoons vegetable oil
- 3 teaspoons applesauce
- 1/2 cup vegetables -- what ever you like
- 1 clove garlic --crushed
- 1 cup whole wheat flour nonfat milk

Mix cheese, oil and applesauce together. Add veggies, garlic,and flour. Combine thoroughly. Add just enough milk to help form a ball. Coverand chill for one hour. Roll onto a floured surface and cut into shapes. Bake in a preheated375 degree oven for 15 minutes or until golden brown. Let cool.

Cheese And Garlic Dog Cookies

- 1 1/2 cups whole wheat flour
- 1 1/4 cups cheddar cheese --grated
- 1/4 pound margarine -- corn oil
- 1 clove garlic --crushed
- 1 Pinch salt

Cream the cheese with the softened margarine, garlic, salt, and flour. Add enough milk to form into a ball. Chill for 1/2 hour. Roll onto floured board. Cut into shapes and bake at 375 for 15 minutes or until slightly brown, and firm.

MAKES 2 to 3 dozen, depending on size.

Cheese N Garlic Bites

- 1 cup wheat flour
- 1 cup cheddar cheese --grated
- 1 tablespoon garlic powder
- 1 tablespoon butter --softened
- 1/2 cup milk

Mix flour and cheese together. Add garlic powder and softenedbutter. Slowly add milk

till you form a stiff dough. You may not need all of the milk.Knead on floured board for a few minutes. Roll out to 1/4 inch thickness. Cut into shapesandplace on ungreased cookie sheet. Bake 350 degrees oven for 15 minutes. Let coolinoven with the door slightly open until cold and firm. Refrigerate to keep fresh.

Cheesey Dog Cookies

- 2 cups All-Purpose flour --un-sifted
- 1 1/4 cups cheddar cheese --shredded
- 2 cloves Garlic -- finely chopped
- 1/2 cup Vegetable oil
- 4 tablespoons Water --(4 to 5)

Combine everything except water. Whisk in food processor until consistency of

cornmeal. Then add water until mixture forms a ball. Roll it into 1/2" thickness and cut into shapes. Bake on ungreased cookie sheets about 10 min. (depending on size of shapes) at 400. Cool and store in refrigerator.

Cheesy Carrot Muffins

- 1 cup all-purpose flour
- 1 cup whole wheat flour
- 1 tablespoon baking powder
- 1 cup cheddar cheese --Shredded
- 1 cup carrot --grated
- 2 large eggs
- 1 cup milk

Preheat oven to 350 degrees. Grease a muffin tin or line it with paper baking cups.

Combine the flours and baking powder and mix well. Add the cheese and carrots and use your fingers to mix them into the flour until they are well-distributed. In another bowl, beat the eggs. Then whisk in the milk and vegetable oil. Pour this over the flour mixture and stir gently until just combined. Fill the muffin cups three-quarters full with the mixture. Bake for 20-25 minutes or until the muffins feel springy. Be sure to let the muffins cool before letting your dog do any taste testing! Onemuffin for medium to large dog, half a muffin for a toy or small dog.

Chicken Garlic Birthday Cake

- 1 chicken bouillon cube
- 1 cup Whole-wheat flour
- 2 cups Wheat germ
- 1/2 cup Cornmeal
- 2 Eggs
- 1/2 cup Vegetable oil
- 1 tablespoon Minced garlic
- 2 cups water vegetable oil spray -- Garlic Flavor

Preheat oven to 375 degrees. Dissolve bouillon cube in warm water. Combine flour, wheat germ, cornmeal, eggs, oil, garlic and water. Spray two cake pans with garlic-flavored oil, and sprinkle with flour. Bake 50 minutes. After removing cake from oven, turn upside down and let cool.

MAKES two small cakes

Classic Canine Cookies

- 4 cups whole wheat flour
- 1/4 cup cornmeal
- 1/4 cup cooked rice
- 1 egg
- 2 tablespoons vegetable oil
- Juice from a small orange
- 1 2/3 cups water

Mix all ingredients together well. Turn out onto a lightly floured surface and knead. Roll out dough to about 1/8 inch thickness and cut out desired shapes... doggy bones, paws, balls, etc... have fun!

Cookie Dipping Sauce:

#1

- 3 cups vanilla chips
- 1 Tbsp. spinach powder
- 1 tsp. garlic powder
- 1 tsp. vegetable oil

#2

- 3 cups carob chips
- 1 tsp. vegetable oil
- 1 tsp. turmeric powder

Melt chips in a double boiler or microwave. Add oils and seasonings. Dip tips of cookies, when cooled, into desired sauce and place on a pan lined withwax paper until set.

Corgi Crumpets

- 2 1/2 cups cornmeal
- 1 1/2 cups cake flour
- 2 tablespoons vegetable oil
- 1 egg
- 2/3 cup honey
- 1/2 teaspoon baking powder
- 1/2 teaspoon cinnamon
- 1/2 teaspoon nutmeg
- 1 small apple
- 1 1/3 cups water
- 1/2 cup rolled oats

Preheat oven to 350. In a bowl, mix all ingredients except the apple and rolled oats. Grate apple into mixture. With an ice cream scoop, fill into muffin pans lined with paper baking cups and sprinkle with oats. Bake for 40 minutes.

Darlene's Favorite Dog Cookie

- 2 cups rye flour
- 1/2 cup vegetable oil
- 2/3 cup warm water
- 1/2 cup white flour
- 1/4 cup cornmeal

Mix well. I usually add about 1/4 tsp. either vanilla or mint flavor.

Roll out to 1/4" thick. Cut into shapes (I usually use about a 3-4" bone-shape cutter). Bake on lightly greased cookie sheet for 30 minutes at 350 degrees.

Dixie's Delights

- 1 ripe banana
- 1/2 cup peanut butter
- 1/4 cup wheat germ
- 1/4 cup unsalted peanuts --chopped

In a small bowl, mash banana and peanut butter together using a fork. Mix in wheat germ. Place in refrigerator for about an hour until, firm. With your hands, roll rounded teaspoonfuls of mixture into balls. Roll balls in peanuts, coating them evenly. Place on cookie sheet in freezer. When completely frozen, pack into airtight containers and store in freezer.

You may want to double this recipe so your pet can share!

Dog and Cat Mini Cakes

- 2 cups whole wheat flour
- 1/2 cup soybean flour
- 1 cup skim milk -- or water
- 1 tablespoon honey
- 1 tablespoon canola oil --or sunflower
- 1 teaspoon sea salt

Mix dry ingredients. Add liquid and honey. Mix and let the dough rest in a warm place for 15 minutes. Add oil and allow to sit another 1/2 hour. Takewalnut size portions of dough and flatten into small cakes. Bake in oven at 400 for 1/2hour.

Dog Bones

- 2 1/4 cups whole wheat flour
- 1/2 cup nonfat dry milk
- 1 egg
- 1/2 cup vegetable oil
- 1 beef bouillon cube
- 1/2 cup hot water
- 1 Tablespoon brown sugar

Preheat the oven to 300 degrees.

In a large mixing bowl, combine all ingredients, stirring until well blended. Knead dough 2 minutes.

On a floured surface, use a floured rolling pin to roll out dough to 1/4-inch thickness.

Using a bone shaped cookie cutter cut out bones.

Bake 30 minutes on an ungreased baking sheet. Remove frompan and cool on wire rack.

Dog Cookies

- 1 c Beef, chicken, or vegetable -stock
- 1 c Bread or all-purpose flour
- 1 c Whole wheat or rye (or other -dark) flour
- 1 c Bulgar wheat
- 1/4 c Non-fat dry milk powder
- 1/2 ts Salt
- 1 1/2 ts Yeast

Use dough cycle. Roll dough to 1/4" thickness. Cut with cookie cutters or knife. Place on baking sheets sprinkled with cornmeal. Cover with clean kitchen towels and let rise in warm place about 45 minutes. Bake at 325-degrees for 45 minutes. When all are baked, turn off oven and return all cookies to cooling oven overnight to harden. Store in airtight container.
(Using a 3.5" bone shaped cutter, you'll get about 30-35 cookies from this recipe.)

Dog Cookies With Chicken Broth

- 2 cups whole wheat flour
- 2/3 cup yellow cornmeal
- 1/2 cup sunflower seeds --shelled
- 2 tablespoons corn oil
- 1/2 cup chicken broth
- 2 eggs
- 1/4 cup low-fat milk
- 1 egg -- beaten

Heat oven to 350 degrees. In a large bowl, mix together flour,cornmeal and seeds. Add oil, broth and egg mixture. The dough should be firm. Let sit15-20 minutes. On a lightly floured surface, roll out dough 1/4 inch thick. Cut into shapesand brush with beaten egg. Bake for 25-35 minutes, until golden brown. Remove and cool.Store in airtight container.

Dog Pooch Munchies

- 3 cups Whole wheat flour
- 1 cup Milk
    - 1 teaspoon Garlic salt
    1/2 cup Soft bacon fat
    1 cup Shredded cheese
    1 Egg --beaten slightly

1. Preheat oven to 400 F. degrees.

2. Place flour and garlic salt in a large bowl. Stir in bacon fat. Add cheese and egg. Gradually add enough milk to form a dough. Knead dough and roll out to about 1 inch thick.
3.Use dog bone cookie cutter to cut out dough. Place on greased cookie sheet. Bake about 12 minutes, until they start to brown. Cool and serve.

Doggie Bone Treats

- 1 cup all-purpose flour
- 1 cup whole wheat flour
- 1/2 cup wheat germ
- 1/2 cup nonfat dry milk
- 3 tablespoons vegetable shortening
- 1 teaspoon brown sugar
- 1/2 teaspoon salt
- 1 egg
- 1/3 cup water

Preheat the oven to 350 degrees.

Coat a cookie sheet with nonstick cooking spray. In a large bowl, combine both flours, wheat germ, nonfat dry milk, shortening, brown sugar, and salt; mix until crumbly. Add the egg and water; mix well.

On a lightly floured surface, knead the dough until smooth. Using a rolling pin, roll out to a 1/2-inch thickness. Using a dog bone-shaped cookie cutter or a knife, cut out biscuits. Place on the cookie sheet and bake for 25 to 30 minutes, or until lightly browned.

Remove to a wire rack to cool completely. Of course, beware of any of your dog's possible allergies to wheat, eggs, or dairy products.

NOTE: I know dogs love these treats because we tested themwith real dogs, who couldn't get enough of them! And don't worry if the kids (oreven adults) get into them. They're perfectly edible - but not very tasty - for humans.

Doggy Dip

- 3 tablespoons peanut butter
- 2 tablespoons honey
- 1 banana --*See Note
- 16 ounces vanilla yogurt
- 1 tablespoon whole wheat flour

Mix the peanut butter, honey, and fruit together until well blended. In a separate bowl, combine the yogurt and flour, mix well. Add the fruit mixture to the yogurt and blend together. Keep cold in refrigerator.

Use this dip to coat or dip biscuits and treats into. Allow treats to chill in refrigerator until coating is set and firm; this prevents big messes!

Note: Very Ripe, or a large jar of baby food fruit, any flavor

Fido's Favorite Treats

- 1 cup oatmeal 1/3 cup butter 1
- teaspoon beef bouillon granules 1/2
- cup hot water 3/4 cup powdered
- milk 3 /4 cup cornmeal 1 egg --
- beaten 3 cups whole wheat flour
-
-
-

Combine oatmeal, butter, and bouillon granules in a large bowl. Pour hot water over this and let stand for 5 minutes. Stir in powdered milk, cornmeal, and egg. Add flour 1/2 c. at a time, mixing well after each addition. Knead for 3-4 minutes, adding more flour if needed to make a very stiff dough. Pat or roll out dough to 1/2" thickness, then cut into bone shaped pieces. Place in a greased baking sheet. Bake at 325* for 50 minutes. Allow to cool and dry out till hard.

Frozen Peanut Butter Yogurt Treats

- 32 ounces vanilla yogurt
- 1 cup peanut butter

1. Put the peanut butter in a microwave safe dish and microwave until melted.

2. Mix the yogurt and the melted peanut butter in a bowl.

3. Pour mixture into cupcake papers and freeze.

Fruity Yogurt Treats

- 2 kiwi fruit -- mashed, or jar baby food fruit
- 8 ounces strawberry yogurt -- or other

Mix together, freeze in ice cube tray. serve.

Good for You Gobblers

- 1 cup white flour
- 1 cup whole wheat flour
- 1/4 cup sunflower seeds --chopped
- 2 tablespoons applesauce
- 1 tablespoon peanut butter
- 1/4 cup molasses
- 2 egg -- beaten
- 1/4 cup milk

Mix the dry ingredients (flour and seeds) together. Add applesauce, peanut butter and molasses and stir well. In a separate bowl mix the egg and milk together. Add to the dough. Add a little more milk if the mixture is too dry you want a firm dough. Knead for a few minutes. Roll out to 1/2" thickness. Cut into desired shapes. Bakes at 350 degrees for 30 minutes, or until biscuits are brown and firm.

Healthy Snacks

- 1 cup white rice flour
- 1/4 cup soy flour
- 1/4 cup egg substitute
- 1 tablespoon molasses --unsulphered
- 1/3 cup milk
- 1/3 cup powdered milk
- 2 tablespoons safflower oil

Preheat oven to 350 degrees. Mix dry ingredients together. Add molasses, egg, oil and milk. Roll out flat onto oiled cookie sheet and cut into dally bite-sized pieces. Bake for 20 minutes. Let cool and store in tightly sealed container.

Home Made Party Cake

- 2/3 cup ripe mashed bananas
- 1/2 cup softened butter
- 3 large eggs
- 3/4 cup water
- 2 cups Unbleached Flour
- 2 teaspoons baking powder
- 1 teaspoon baking soda
- 2 teaspoons cinnamon
- 1/2 cup chopped pecans
- 1/2 cup raisins

Frosting:
- 2 cup mashed banana
- 1 tablespoon butter
- 6 tablespoon carob flour
- 2 teaspoons vanilla
- 3 tablespoon unbleached flour
- 1 teaspoon cinnamon

Cake:
In mixing bowl, beat together mashed banana and butter until creamy. Add eggs and water. Beat well. Stir in dry ingredients. Beat until smooth. Add nuts and raisins. Spoon batter evenly into oiled and floured bundt pan. Bake at 350 degrees for about 35 minutes. Cool on wire rack 5 minutes, remove from pan, replace on rack and cool.

Frosting:

Blend thoroughly and spread on cool cake. Sprinkle with chopped pecans. The frosting contains carob, which is a safe (almost tastes like) chocolate substitute.

Homemade Liver Treats

- 1 cup whole wheat flour
- 1 cup cornmeal
- 1/2 cup wheat germ
- 1 teaspoon garlic powder
- 1 pound beef liver

Pre-heat oven to 350.

Liquefy liver in blender, add dry ingredients. Grease cookie sheet. Drop teaspoonfuls of mixture onto cookie sheet and flatten with bottom of glass dipped in water and cornmeal. Bake for 15-20 minutes.
You may store baked or unbaked dough in freezer. This makesa big batch, so share some. They smell absolutely wonderful to dogs. Your familymake not like the smell of them baking. I use these for bait for show ring.

Icy Paws

- 2 cartonsplainorvanillayogurt (32 oz each)
- 1 smallcantunainwater(8oz.)
- 2 tsp.garlicpower
- 24 3oz.plasticcups(notpaper)

Open yogurt,iftheyarefulltothetop use a spoon & scoop out one cup. (these will be frozen as plainyogurt).Puthalfofthe can of tuna in each yogurt container add the garlic power (1 tsp.ineach)&stirthoroughly.

Use a spoon&scoopthemixtureinto the cups. Place on a tray & freeze overnight. Makesabout24treats.

VARIATIONS:
Mix in garlicpowder,brewersyeast& fennel seed. Veggie Delight: Mix in cooked peas or other vegetables.

Chicken IcyPaws:usecannedchicken instead of tuna
Potassium Boost:Addinamashedbanana.

Lab Liver-Chip Cookie

- 2 cups Whole wheat flour
- 1/3 cup Butter --melted
- 1 Egg --beaten
- 6 tablespoons Water
- 1/4 cup liver --dried or jerky-style treats --chopped

Preheat oven to 350 degrees. Combine flour, butter, egg, and water. Mix well. Blend in liver bits. Turn onto a greased baking pan. Bake 20 to 25 minutes. Cool and cut.

Liver Brownies

- 1lb. chicken or beef liver -I prefer the chicken livers, they don't seem to smell as bad
- ½ lb. PLAIN cornmeal (non rising)
- ½ lb. plain old-fashioned oatmeal
- 1 can salmon or mackerel (with juice)
- 1 Cup chicken broth or water
- 1 Tablespoon minced garlic
- 1 egg
- Dash of salt
- ¼ Cup parsley flakes

Place liver, egg, fish, broth, garlic, salt and parsley flakes inablender or food processor and blend until smooth. Mix corn and oatmeal's, and then addliver mixture. Mix well. Once mixed, batter should be like a slightly wet brownie mix.Add more broth or water if necessary. Pour mixture onto well-greased cookie sheet andbake at 250 degrees for 1 ½ to2 hours. Cut into squares while still warm. Cool, and thenfreeze what you won't use in 1week or less.

Liver Treats

1poundbeef liver Allyou need are beef livers. Try your local meat packers; they often throw them away. Oryou can buy fresh liver from the supermarket. Cut the liver into approximately 1 inch slices. Place in your food dehydrator for 24 hours*. Use Pam or the equivalent on the drying racks, so the liver won't stick. Let dry for 24 hours. *Or you could place them on a cookie sheet and bake in a 325degree oven for about 45 minutes to help dry them out.

Liver Treats For Dogs

- 1 pound beef liver
- 2 garlic cloves
- 1 Box corn muffin mix

Preheat oven to temperature in corn muffin directions.

Mix liver and garlic in a blender or food processor, then process till liquid. Stir in muffin mix, then scrape onto a baking sheet and pat to app. 1/2-1" thickness. Bake till very firm, but not burned.

Cut into squares, then store in refrigerator or freezer.

Lucy's Liver Slivers

- 1/2 pound chicken livers -- cooked
- 1 cup chicken stock
- 1/2 cup corn oil
- 1 tablespoon chopped parsley
- 1 cup powdered milk
- 1 cup rolled oats
- 1/2 cup brewer's yeast
- 1 cup soy flour
- 1 cup cornmeal
- 3 cups whole wheat flour

Preheat oven to 350°. In food processor or blender, process chicken livers, chicken stock, corn oil and parsley until smooth. Transfer to large bowl. Add powdered milk, rolled oats, brewer's yeast, soy flour and cornmeal. Mix well. Gradually add whole wheat flour. You'll have to use your hands here, kneading in as much of the flour as it takes to create a very stiff dough.

Roll dough out to 1/4" thick and cut into stick shapes, about1/2" by 4" (depending on the size of your dog). A pizza cutter works great! Bake on ungreased cookie sheet for 20 to 25 minutes until lightly browned and crisp. Turn off heat andlet biscuits dry out in oven for several hours. Store in the refrigerator.

Massive Mastiff Munchy Muffins

- 2 carrots
- 2 3/4 cups water
- 1 egg
- 1/4 teaspoon vanilla extract
- 2 tablespoons honey
- 1 1/2 banana --*see Note
- 4 cups whole wheat flour
- 1 tablespoon baking powder
- 1 tablespoon cinnamon
- 1 tablespoon nutmeg

Shred the carrot with a hand shredder or in a blender. Mix all wet ingredients together in a bowl, then add the pureed banana. Mix together thoroughly. Set aside. Combine the dry ingredients. Add the wet ingredients to the dry and mix thoroughly, leaving no dry mixture on the bottom. Coat a 12 muffin pan with nonstick spray. Fill each muffin hole 3/4 full. Bake about 1 hour at 350 degrees.
Note: over ripe. Try replacing the banana with one apple for a different flavor!

Munchie Crunchy Meat Treats

* 1/2 cup powdered milk -- non-fat
* 1 egg -- beaten
* 1 1/2 cups rice flour
* 1/2 teaspoon honey
* 1/2 cup water
* 5 teaspoons chicken broth -- or beef
* 1 jar baby food, meat, beef, strained -- meat, any flavor

Combine all ingredients well. Form into a ball. Roll dough out on a floured surface. Cut out desired shapes. Bake in a 350 degree oven for 25-30 minutes. Let cool. The treats should be hard and crunchy.

Peanut Butter & Oats Glazed Goodies

* 1 cup water
* 1 cup quick cooking oats
* 1/4 cup butter --half stick
* 1/2 cup cornmeal
* 1 tablespoon sugar
* 1 teaspoon salt
* 1/2c up milk
* 1/3cup peanut butter
* 3cups whole wheat flour
*

Boilwaterin a saucepan. Add oats and butter. Let oats soak for ten minutes. Stir in the cornmeal,sugar, salt, milk, peanut butter, and egg. Mix thoroughly. Add the flour, one cupatatime (you may not need the entire amount) until a stiff dough forms. Kneaddough on floured surface until smooth, about 3 minutes. Roll to 1/2" thickness. Placeonagreased cookie sheet.

Glaze:

* 1large egg
* 2tbsp. milk

Mixwell.Brush glaze on dough with a pastry brush. Bake inapre-heated 325 degree ovenfor35-45 minutes or until golden brown. Cool completely.

Peanut Butter Cookies

- 2 cups whole wheat flour
- 1 cup wheat germ
- 1 cup peanut butter
- 1 egg
- 1/4 cup vegetable oil
- 1/2 cup water
- 1/2 teaspoon salt

Preheat oven to 350 degrees F.

Combine flour wheat germ and salt in large bowl then mix in peanut butter, egg oil and water. Roll dough out onto a lightly floured surface till about 1/2 inch thick...then cut out the biscuits using a cookie cutter --(or make squares). Put the biscuits onto an ungreased baking sheet. Bake 15 mins for the smaller sized cookies and up to 35 mins. for larger shaped ones.

Store in the fridge ...if they last that long!!!!!

Pet Party Mix

- 2 cups Cheerios®
- 2 cups Chex mix
- 2 teaspoons gravy, dry mix, brown
- 1/2 cup Bacos®
- 2 cups Shredded Wheat® -- spoon size
- 1/2 cup melted butter -- or margarine
- 1/2 cup American Cheese --grated
- 1 pieces Beef Jerky -- dog treats (pupperoni, Jerky Treats, etc.)

1. Preheat oven to 275 .

2. Pour melted butter/margarine into a 33x23 cm baking pan. Stir in cheese, bacon bits, and gravy mix. Add cereal and stir until all pieces are coated.

3. Heat until crisp, approx. 45 min.

4. Let cool and store in tightly sealed container.

Pet Puffs

- 1 package Dry yeast
- 1/4 cup Warm water(110-115F.)
- 1 1/2 cups Whole wheat flour
- 1 cup All-Purpose flour
- 1 package Unflavored gelatin
- 1 cup Non-fat dry milk powder
- 1/4 cup Corn oil
- 1 Egg 1 Can pet food --(6 to 8 oz)
- 1/4 cup Water

Dissolve yeast in 1/4 cup warm water. Mix dry ingredients. Add all ingredients together.

(Dough will be very stiff; it may be necessary to mix with your hands.) Drop dough by level half-teaspoons onto ungreased cookie sheet. Bake in a preheated 300F. oven 25 minutes.

Pooch Peanut Butter Swirls

Dough #1 4 cups whole wheatflour 1/2 cup cornmeal 1 1/3 cups water 1/3 cup peanut butter 1 egg Dough #2 4 cups whole wheat flour 2/3 cup cornmeal 1/2 cup banana -- mashed 1 egg 1 1/4 cups water 2 tablespoons vegetable oil 2 tablespoons molasses 2 tablespoons cinnamon Combine all #1 ingredients and mix thoroughly. Knead on a lightly floured surface. Set aside. Combine all #2 ingredients and mix thoroughly. Knead on a lightly floured surface. Roll each dough separately to a 1/8 inch thickness, into rectangles. Lightly brush a little water over the top of the light dough. Place the dark dough on top, then roll up like a jelly roll. Wrap the roll in plastic and chill in the freezer for one hour. Cut the roll into 1/4 inch slices. Place them on a cookie sheet sprayed with non-stick spray. Bake at 350 degrees for one hour.

Poochie Pint-Sized Carrot Treats

- 1/2 cup cheddar cheese --shredded
- 1/4 cup margarine --half stick
- 1 drop red food coloring -- or more if needed
- 1 drop yellow food coloring -- or more if needed
- 1 jar baby food carrots
- 1 cup all-purpose flour
- 1/2 garlic powder
- 1/4 cup milk -- or more if needed

Melt cheese and margarine in a saucepan, stirring frequently.Take off heat. Stir in food dye, to make orange color. Add carrots, flour, and garlic powder.Stir until well blended. Add enough milk to form into a ball. Transfer to a mixing bowland chill for one hour. Roll dough on a lightly floured, flat surface to 1/4" thickness.Place on a cookie sheet lightly sprayed with nonfat cooking spray. Bake in a preheated350 degree oven for 20 - 30 minutes, or until golden brown. Cool completely.

Rover's Reward

- 1 package active dry yeast
- 1 teaspoon sugar
- 2 cups all-purpose flour
- 2 cups whole-wheat flour
- 2 cups cornmeal
- 2 cups oatmeal --uncooked
- 1 cup fresh mint leaves -- chopped, loose packed
- 1 cup parsley sprigs -- chopped, loose packed
- 1/2 cup toasted wheat germ
- 1 can beef broth --(13 3/4 to 14 1/2 ounces)
- 3/4 cup milk

1. Preheat oven to 350 degrees F. In small bowl, combine yeast, sugar, and 1/4 cup warm water (105 degrees to 115 degrees F.). Let stand until yeast foams, about 5 minutes.
2. In very large bowl, combine all-purpose flour, whole-wheat flour, cornmeal, oats, mint, parsley, and wheat germ. With wooden spoon, stir in yeast mixture, broth, and milk until combined. With hands, knead dough in bowl until blended, about 1 minute.
3. Divide dough in half. Cover 1 piece with plastic wrap to prevent drying out. Place remaining piece of dough on lightly floured surface. With floured rolling pin, roll dough to 1/4-inch thickness. With large (about 5 inches) or small (about 2 inches) cookie cutter, such as bone* or mailman, cut out as many biscuits as possible, reserving trimmings. With spatula, transfer biscuits to large ungreased cookie sheet. Reroll trimmings and cut more biscuits. Repeat with remaining dough.
4. Bake small biscuits 30 minutes, bake large biscuits 40 minutes. Turn oven off; leave biscuits in oven 1 hour to dry out.
5. Remove biscuits fromcookie sheet to wire rack. When cool, store at room temperature in tightly covered container up to 3 months. Each large biscuit: About 90 calories, 4 g protein, 17 g carbohydrate, 1 g total fat (0 g saturated), 1 mg cholesterol, 30 mg sodium. Make these treats large or small; the dogs in our neighborhood loved them! Do- Ahead: up to 3 months.
Yields: about 4 dozen large biscuits or 24 dozen small biscuitsWork Time: 1 hour plus cooling Total Time: 30 to 40 minutes plus drying.

Salmon Treats

- 1 can salmon, canned, pink
- 1/2 cup chopped parsley
- 3 eggs --shells included
- 1/2 cup sesame seeds -- ground in coffee grinder
- 1/2 cup flax seeds -- ground in coffee grinder
- 2 cups potato flour --(2 to 3)

Put these ingredients into a food processor, mix VERY WELL. Pourpotatoflourthrough the opening while the motor is running. I can't tell you exactlyhowmuch, butIwould guess about 2-3 cups. When the dough forms, like a pie crust, androllsintoaballit is ready to take out. Dump this mess onto potato floured counterorboard. Kneadmore flour into this and when it is a rolled out cookie consistency, itisreadytorolloutinto about 14 inch thick. I use a pizza cutter to roll our long stripsandthencutcrosswise to make small squares . If you want FANCY you may use a cookiecutter. Bakeoncookie sheets, sprayed Pam or line the sheet with parchment paper. Iputinasmanyaswill fit. Usually two whole cookie sheets suffices. I bake this in a 375°ovenfor20min. Turn and rotate the cookie sheets and bake about 10 more minutes. Youcanmakethemassoft or as hard as you want.

Scrumptious Carob Bake

- 6 cups white rice flour
- 1/8 cup peanut oil
- 1/8 cup margarine --safflower oil type
- 1 Tbsp brown sugar
- 4 ounces carob -- chips, melted
- 1 cup water
- 1/4 cup molasses
- 1/2 cup powdered milk

Mix dry ingredients in a large bowl. Add remaining ingredientsand mix until blended. Dough will be stiff. Chill. Roll dough on a greased cookie panand cut into shapes 1/2 inch thick. Bake at 300 for 1 hour.

Sheltie Scones

- 2 1/2 cups self-rising flour
- 1 cup beef liver --chopped
- 1/2 cup water --or beef stock
- 1/2 cup milk
- 2 tablespoons butter
- 1/4 teaspoon salt

(Chopped Liver: Just boil the liver until it is gray and a rubbery consistency. Or if you have a microwave, cook it on high for about 8 mins. Chop it up into small pieces and when cool put the pieces into a number of airtight bags and store in the fridge. Use liver pieces as treats when training)

Scones: Sift flour and salt into a bowl, rub in butter. Add chopped liver. Use a knife to stir in milk and enough water to mix to a sticky dough. Turn dough onto lightly floured surface, knead quickly and lightly until dough is smooth. Press dough out evenly to about 2 cm and cut into rounds. Place on prepared tray and bake in very hot over for 15 minutes.

Makes about 16-18.

Snickerpoodles Dog Treats

- 1/2 cup vegetable oil
- 1/2 cup shortening
- 1 cup honey
- 2 eggs
- 3 3/4 cups white flour
- 2 teaspoons cream of tartar
- 1 teaspoon baking soda
- 1/2 cup cornmeal
- 2 teaspoons cinnamon

Mix vegetable oil, shortening and honey together until smooth. Add eggs and beat well.

Blend in flour, baking soda and cream of tartar. Knead dough until mixed well. Shape dough by rounded teaspoons into balls. Mix the cornmeal and cinnamon together in a bowl and roll balls in mixture. Place 2 inches apart on a cookie sheet that has been sprayed with a nonstick spray. Press the balls down with a fork twice going in 2 different directions or press with your favorite stamp. Bake 8 minutes at 400. Remove from baking sheet and cool on a rack.

Pasta recipe. form into the desired ravioli shape and size. Cover with damp cloth and set aside.

In a bowl, mix yogurt, whole wheat flour and eggs. Add salmon and parsley mix a few more moments.

Depending on ravioli size, place 1 to 4 teaspoons in center of each, moisten edges and fold.

Ravioli can be boiled or baked. If boiling, place in rapid boiling water for 10 to 15 minutes or till done. If baking pre-heat oven to 375, place ravioli on a baking sheet, put in oven for 20 to 25 minutes.

Note: use leftover meat such as beef, chicken, lamb etc. Alsoshredded veggies like carrots, sweet potato, etc. or chopped veggies such as greenbeans, broccoli, kale etc. raw oat meal and cooked rice or cooked barley, can be used in placeof meat.

Surprise Snacks

- 1/4 cup hot water
- 8 chicken bouillon cube -- or beef
- 1 package dry yeast
- 1 1/2 cups tomato juice
- 2 cups flour --divided
- 2 cups wheat germ
- 1 1/2 cups whole wheat flour

Place the hot water and bouillon cubes in a large mixing bowlandmashwithafork.

Sprinkle yeast over this mixture and let stand about 5 minutes,untilyeastisdissolved. Add the tomato juice, half the flour and the wheat germ and stirtoformasmoothbatter. Gradually work in the remaining flour and the whole wheat flourwithyourhands.Divide the dough into 4 balls. Roll each ball out on a floured board toabout1/4"thick.Cutinto shapes and place on ungreased cookie sheets about an inch apart.Bakeina3250F.oven for 1 hour, then turn off the heat and let biscuits dry in oven forabout4hoursor overnight with the door propped open slightly. Store in airtightcontainer.

Tempting Training Treats

- 2 1/3 cups flour -- all-purpose or whole wheat
- 1/4 cup olive oil
- 1/4 cup applesauce
- 1/2 cup grated cheese --like parmesan
- 1 large egg
- 1 teaspoon garlic powder
- 1/4 cup powdered milk -- non-fat

Combine all ingredients in a large bowl; mix well; Roll the dough out to size of a cookie sheet; Pat the dough onto a lightly greased cookie sheet, bringing it to the edges. Using a sharp knife or a pizza cutter, cut desired sizes into dough (justscore through). If you're using as training treats, cut them into small pieces; Sprinklealittle extra cheese and garlic powder if desired on dough for flavor. Bake in a 350degree oven about 15 minutes until golden brown. Turn off the oven and let cool for a fewhours; They will keep hardening the longer you leave them. Break them apart; storetightly covered or in the freezer.

Tess' Tantalizing Treats

- 1 cup oatmeal --quick
- 1/4 cup margarine
- 1 1/2 cups hot water
- 1/2 cup powdered milk
- 1 cup grated cheddar cheese --or Swiss, Colby
- 1/4 teaspoon garlic powder
- 1 egg -- beaten
- 1 cup cornmeal
- 1 cup wheat germ
- 3 cups whole wheat flour
- 1 tablespoon beef bouillon -- or chicken

1.Preheat oven to 300°.
2.In large bowl pour hot water over oatmeal and margarine (cut-up melts faster); let stand 5 minutes. Stir in powdered milk, grated cheese, garlic powder, bouillon and egg. Add cornmeal and wheat germ. Mix well. Add flour, 1/2 cup at a time, mixing well after each addition. Knead 3-4 minutes, adding more flour if necessary to make very stiff dough. Pat or roll dough to 1/2 inch thickness.
3.Cut into bone shaped biscuits and place on a greased baking sheet. Bake for 1 hour. Turn off heat and leave in oven an additional 1 1/2 hours or longer.
Makes approximately 2 1/4 pounds.

Turkey Treats

- 2 cups cooked turkey -- cut up
- 2 cloves garlic
- 4 teaspoons grated cheese
- 1 tablespoon parsley --freshly chopped
- 2 egg
- 2 cups whole wheat flour
- 2 tablespoons brewer's yeast
- 2 tablespoons vegetable oil

Combine turkey, garlic, cheese, parsley and mix well. Beat theeggs in a bowl and pour over turkey mixture. Add the flour, yeast, and oil. Stir until thoroughly mixed and all ingredients are coated. Drop into small lumps onto ungreasedcookie sheet. Cook in a 350 degree oven for about 20 minutes, until brown and firm. Storein refrigerator.

Veggie Bones

- 3 cups minced parsley
- 1/4 cup carrots --shredded
- 1/4 cup shredded mozzarella cheese
- 2 tablespoons olive oil
- 2 3/4 cups all-purpose flour
- 2 tablespoons bran
- 2 teaspoons baking powder
- 1/2 cup water --possibly more

Preheat oven to 350 F, rack on middle level. Lightly grease a baking sheet.
Stir together parsley, carrots, cheese, and oil. Combine all the dry ingredients and add to the veggies. Gradually add 1/2 cup of water, mixing well. Make a moist, but not wet dough. If needed add a little more water. Knead for one minute.
Roll out dough to 1/2 inch thickness. Using cookie cutter, cut out the shapes and transfer them to a baking sheet. Reroll the scraps and continue until dough is all used up.
Bake for 20 to 30 minutes until biscuits have browned and hardened slightly. They will harden more as they cool. Store in an airtight container.

Wacky Wheat Treats

- 2 jars baby food, meat, beef, strained -- *see Note
- 1/2 cup nonfat dry milk
- 2 ounces wheat germ
- 1/3 cup water
- 1/2 cup flour
- 1 teaspoon garlic powder

Mix together well. Roll out dough on floured surface. Cut out witch hat patterns and place on lightly greased cookie sheet.
Bake in a 325 degree oven until golden brown, about 30-35 minutes.
Note: chicken, lamb, beef, etc.. - you choose.

Puppy
PuppyFormulas
Recipe #1

2/3 Cup Goat milk canned (or just regular canned milk)
1/3 Cup water or Pedialyte
1 teaspoon Karo Syrup
1 egg yolk 1 teaspoon Dyne or pediatric vitamin
Strain a couple of times to make sure there is no albumin in the mixture, although it has been used successfully without egg at all.
Variation: 1 can of Condensed Milk rather than goat's milk (it may be too high in protein and put a strain on the puppy's kidneys 1 envelope of Knox unflavored gelatin in addition to other ingredients (helps keep stools solid).

Recipe #2

- 1 cup of canned Condensed milk or evaporated milk
- 4 ounces plain, full-fat yogurt
- 1 egg yolk
- 1 dropper full of baby vitamins

Mix well.

Recipe #3

- 2 cups hot water
- 1 can Evaporated milk (Not condensed--both are in bakery section of store but different products)
- 2 eggs
- 3 tablespoons Karo syrup
- 2 envelopes Knox unflavored gelatin.

Mix thoroughly to get the gelatin working.

Recipe #4

4ounces Carnation EVAPORATED milk
4ounces FULL FAT natural, plain yogurt
1tablespoon Mayonnaise, (NOT salad dressing and definitely NOT DIET)
1egg yolk
1dropper full of human baby pediatric liquid vitamin, no fluoride.
Whiz in blender...feed baby.

Puppy Pretzels

- 1 teaspoon brown sugar
- 2 teaspoons active dry yeast
- 2/3 cup water
- 3/4 cup whole wheat flour
- 3 tablespoons soy flour, low fat
- 1/4 cup nonfat dry milk
- 1 tablespoon dried liver powder
- 1 tablespoon bone meal flour
- 3/4 teaspoon salt 1 egg -- beaten (1/2 in recipe, 1/2 in glaze)
- 2 tablespoons cooking oil
- 3 tablespoons wheat germ

Dissolve yeast and sugar in warm water.
Combine dry ingredients. Add half of the beaten egg, oil and yeast-water mixture. Mix well.
Knead on a well floured board until dough is firm. Place in oiled bowl, cover and let rise until double in bulk.
Shape into pretzels and place on greased cookie sheet. Bake in preheated 375 degree oven for 15 minutes. Remove and brush with beaten egg and sprinkle with wheat germ. Return to oven and bake at 300 degrees for about 15 minutes until nicely browned and quite firm.
Note: You may omit liver powder and bone meal flour if youhave difficulty locating them.

Yogurt Pups

- 16 ounces plain nonfat yogurt
- 3/4 cup water
- 1 tablespoon chicken bouillon granules

Dissolve bouillon in water, Combine water and yogurt in blender and blend thoroughly, Pour into small containers for freezing, cover and freeze.

Shampoo's/Soap/Oils

Dog Oil Supplement

- 1/4 cup olive oil 1/4
- cup canola oil 1/4
- cup cod liver oil 1/4
- cup flax seed oil

Place oils in brown bottle and shake well. Store in refrigerator.

Add two teaspoons to the dogs food each day. Can be add to dry food as well.

Safflower and Sunflower oil may used as well.

Meals

Alfalfa Hearts

2cupswhole wheatflour 1/2 cup soy flour 1 teaspoon bone meal -- optional 2 tablespoons nutritional yeast 1 tablespoon lecithin --optional 1/2 teaspoon salt 1/4 teaspoon garlic powder 3 tablespoons alfalfa sprouts -- chopped 1 cup brown rice -- cooked 3 tablespoons canola oil 1/2 cup water

Combine flours, bone meal, yeast, lecithin, salt, garlic powder and alfalfa leaves. Add rice and oil. Combine well.

Add 1/4 cup water and mix well. Dough should be very easy to handle, not crumbly. Add more water if needed to achieve proper consistency.

Lightly flour board or counter and roll out dough to 1/4 inch thickness. Cut with 2 1/2 inch cutter. Bake at 350 degrees for 25 minutes.

Makes 3 dozen.

Bacon Bites

- 3 cups whole wheat flour
- 1/2 cup milk
- 1 egg
- 1/4 cup bacon grease -- or vegetable oil
- 1 teaspoon garlic powder
- 4 slices bacon -- crumbled
- 1/2 cup cold water

Mix ingredients together thoroughly. Roll out on a floured surface to 1/2 - 1/4" thickness. Bake for 35-40 minutes in a 325 degree oven.

Bacon Bits for Dogs

- 6 slices cooked bacon -- crumbled
- 4 eggs -- well beaten
- 1/8 cup bacon grease
- 1 cup water
- 1/2 cup powdered milk -- non-fat
- 2 cup graham flour
- 2 cup wheat germ
- 1/2 cup cornmeal

Mix ingredients with a strong spoon; drop heaping tablespoonfuls onto a greased baking sheet. Bake in a 350 oven for 15 minutes. Turn off oven and leave cookies on baking sheet in the oven overnight to dry out.

Baker's Bagels

1cup wholewheat flour 1cup unbleached flour 1package yeast -- 1/4 ounce 1cup chicken broth -- warmed 1tablespoon honey 1.Preheat oven to 375°. 2.In large bowl combine the whole wheat flour with the yeast. Add 2/3 cup chicken broth and honey and beat for about 3 minutes. Gradually add the remaining flour. Knead the dough for a few minutes until smooth and moist, but not wet (use reserve broth as necessary). 3. Cover the dough and let it rest for about 5 minutes.Dividethe dough into about 15-20 pieces, rolling each piece into a smooth ball. Punchaholeintoeach ball with your finger or end of spoon and gently pull the dough so the holeisaboutan 1/2" wide. Don't be too fussy here, the little bagels rise into shape when theybake.

4. Place all the bagels on a greased cookie sheet andallowtorise 5 minutes. Bake for 25 minutes. Turn the heat off and allow the bagels to coolintheoven.

BARF Breakfast (med size dog)

- 1/4 cup rolled oats
- 1/2 cup yogurt
- 1/4 cup vegetables -- *see Note
- 250 mgs vitamin C -- for dogs. Crushed
- 1 teaspoon honey
- 1 teaspoon apple cider vinegar
- 1 teaspoon kelp seaweed powder -- *see Note
- 1 teaspoon alfalfa powder -- *see Note
- 1 digestive enzyme -- for dogs Optional
- 1 teaspoon flax seed oil -- *see Note
- 1/4 cup kibble -- optional

Soak rolled oats in yogurt overnight. Mix all ingredients and serve. Add kibble if desired.

Note: shredded, lightly steamed or pureed. carrots, celery, spinach, yams and/or broccoli, apples etc.

Note: items can be purchased at health food store or pet store.

BARF Dinner (med size dog)

- 3/4 pound Raw Meat -- *see Note
- 1 egg -- raw
- 1/2 clove garlic -- chopped
- 2 tablespoons yogurt
- 1 teaspoon honey
- 1 tablespoon apple cider vinegar
- 1/2 teaspoon flax seed oil -- *see Note
- 1 teaspoon kelp seaweed powder -- *see Note
- 1 teaspoon alfalfa powder -- *see Note
- 250 mgs vitamin C -- for dogs
- 1/4 cup kibble -- optional

Mix together and serve.

*Note: raw beef chunks (not ground), raw chicken, mackerel, or lamb etc. twice a week use liver or kidney.
Note: found in health food store or pet store

Barking Barley Brownies

- 1 1/4 pounds beefliver--or chicken liver
- 2 cups wheat germ
- 2 tablespoons whole wheat flour
- 1 cup cooked barley
- 2 whole eggs
- 3 tablespoons peanut butter
- 1 clove garlic
- 1 tablespoon olive oil
- 1 teaspoon salt --optional

Pre heat oven to 350.
Liquefy liver and garlic clove in a blender, when its smooth add eggs and peanut butter. Blend till smooth.
In separate mixing bowl combine wheat germ, whole wheat flour, and cooked Barley.
Add processed liver mixture, olive oil and salt. Mix well. spread mixture in a greased 9x9 baking dish. Bake for 20 minutes or till done.
When cool cut into pieces that accommodate your doggies size.
Store in refrigerator or freezer.

Basenji Stew

- 4 small parsnip -- **see Note 2 whole yellow
- squash -- cubed 2 whole Sweet potatoes -- peeled
- and cubed 2 whole Zucchini -- cubed 5 whole
- tomatoes -- canned 1 can garbanzo beans, canned -
- - *see Note 15 oz 1/2 cup Couscous 1/4 cup
- Raisins 1 teaspoon Ground coriander 1/2 teaspoon
- Ground turmeric 1/2 teaspoon Ground cinnamon
- 1/2 teaspoon Ground ginger 1/4 teaspoon Ground
- cumin 3 cups Water -- *see Note
-
-
-
-
-

** kohlrabi may be substituted for the parsnips.
*Chick-peas
*or 3 cups chicken stock
Combine all the ingredients in a large saucepan. Bring to a boil, lower the heat, and simmer until the vegetables are tender, about 30 minutes.
Place over cook brown rice or barley

Beef and Rice Moochies

- 1 jar babyfood, dinner, vegetables and beef, strained
- 2 1/2 cups flour, all-purpose
- 1 cup whole wheat flour
- 1 cup rice
- 1 package unflavored gelatin
- 1 whole egg
- 2 tablespoons vegetable oil
- 1 cup powdered milk
- 1 package yeast
- 1/4 cup warm water
- 1 beef bouillon cube

Dissolve yeast in warm water. Mix dry ingredients in large bowl. Add yeast, egg, oil, baby food and dissolved beef bouillon. Mix well. Mixture will be very dry, knead with hands until it forms a ball. Roll out on floured surface to 1/4 inch thickness, cut in 1 or 2 inch circles. Bake on un-greased cookie sheet 30 minutes at 300 degrees.
Store in refrigerator.

Beef Twists

- 3 1/2 cups flour, all-purpose
- 1 cup cornmeal
- 1 package unflavored gelatin
- 1/4 cup milk
- 1 egg
- 1/4 cup corn oil
- 1 jar Baby food, meat, beef, strained
- 1 beef bouillon cube
- 3/4 cup boiling water -- or beef stock

Dissolve bouillon cube in water. Sift dry ingredients in large bowl. Add milk, egg, oil, beef and beef bouillon. Stir until well mixed. Roll out on a floured surface to 1/4 inch thickness. Cut in 1/4 inch by 3 inch strips, twisting each stick 3 turns before placing on cookie sheet. Bake 35-40 minutes at 400 degrees.
Store in refrigerator.

Bow Wow Burritos

1tablespoon oil
12ounces cooked beef -- *see Note
1clovegarlic --minced
3tablespoons chunky peanut butter
1cansweet potatoes --(23-oz.) drained
1canblack beans --(15-oz.) rinsed
1teaspoon chili powder
1teaspoon cumin
1/2teaspoon cinnamon
2teaspoons beef bouillon -- powder
6flourtortillas -- (10-inch)
2tablespoons cilantro --chopped
6tablespoons cheese -- shredded
6tablespoons vegetables --*see Note

Heatoilin large skillet over medium heat until hot. Add garlic; cook and stir 2 to 3

minutesor until tender. Stir in peanut butter, sweet potatoes and beans; mash slightly. Addcumin, cinnamon and chili powder, beef bouillon; mix well. Reduce heat to low; add beef,cover and simmer 2 to 3 minutes or until thoroughly heated, stirring occasionally. Meanwhile, heat tortillas according to package directions.

To serve, spoon and spread scant 1/2 cup mixture across center third of each tortilla with

one piece of meat in center.
Top each with 1 tablespoon sour cream, 1 teaspoon cilantro, I tablespoon Cheese spread to cover mixture.

Fold sides of each tortilla 1 inch over filling. Fold bottom 1/3 of tortilla over filling; roll

again to enclose filling.
*Note: Beef or chicken cut into 1/2 inch strips, or "meatless" meat for the vegetarian doggies.
*Note: Optional... Shredded veggies for added nutrition, carrots, green beans, broccoli etc.
Serving Ideas : Add 1 Teaspoon Dog Oil Supplement and 1 teaspoon Dog Powder Mix Supplement for added nutrition before folding burritos.

Canine Meat and Grain Menu

- 2 cups cooked brown rice
- 2/3 cup Lean beef
- 2 teaspoons lard -- or veggie oil
- 1/4 cup vegetables --no onion
- *Supplements

Mix the above. You can cook the meat if you want to, use your judgment. Serve slightly warm.

*For supplements, add 2 tsp. powder and 1 tsp. oil to feed daily- now this is for a 5-15 lb. dog, and the book instructs to use double supplements for a puppy.

Carob Cornered Crunchies
2 1/4 cups whole wheat flour

- 1egg
- 1/4 cup applesauce
- 1/4 cup vegetable oil
- 1 beef bouillon -- or chicken
- 1/2 cup hot water
- 1 tablespoon honey
- 1 tablespoon molasses
- 1 cup carob bar

Mix all ingredients together until well blended. Knead dough two minutes on a lightly floured surface. Roll to 1/4" thickness. Bake on an ungreased cookie sheet for 30 minutes in a 300 degree oven. Cool.

Melt carob chips in microwave or saucepan. Dip cool biscuits in carob or lay on a flat surface and brush carob

over the biscuits with a pastry brush. Let cool.

Chewy Cheesy Chihuahua Pizza

Crust

- 2 cups cake flour
- 1 1/4 cups whole wheat flour
- 1/4 cup olive oil 1 egg
- 1 cup water
- 1 teaspoon baking soda

Sauce & Toppings

- 1 tomato
- 1 cup tomato puree
- 1 clove garlic
- 1/4 cup parmesan cheese --grated
- 1/2 teaspoon oregano
- 1/2 teaspoon basil
- 2/3 cup cooked rice

CRUST: Mix all ingredients together. Knead on a lightly floured surface. Spray a regular sized, 12 " pizza pan with nonstick spray. Next, spread the dough to the edges of the pan, forming a lip around the ends. Set aside.

Sauce & Toppings: In a food processor, blend tomato, tomato puree and garlic. Spoon the mixture over the pizza crust. Sprinkle the cheese and spices evenly over sauce. Cut the pizza into slices with a pizza cutter or sharp knife.

Bake in a 325 degree oven for 25 minutes. Take out and sprinkle rice evenly over pizza. Return to oven and bake 25 minutes more.

Yield: one 12 inch pizza.

Chow Chow Chicken

- 2 chicken thighs -- or white meat
- 1 stalk celery -- sliced thick
- 3 carrot -- peeled and halved
- 2 small potato --peeled and cubed
- 2 cups rice -- uncooked

Place chicken pieces in large pot. Cover with cold water (5 -6cups). Add carrots, celery,

and potatoes to water. Add salt to taste if you want. Cover andsimmer on low heat about 2 hours until the chicken becomes tender. Add the rice, coverand cook over low heat for about 30 minutes until the rice is tender and most of the liquidis absorbed. Remove soup from heat. Pull the chicken meat off the bone (if will practically fall off), discard bones. Return shredded pieces to pot. Stir well. Let cool. Store in therefrigerator or freeze.

Chow Chow Stew

- 1 tablespoon olive oil
- 2 pounds beef --*see Note
- 2 cups cabbage -- chopped
- 3 cloves garlic -- minced, up to
- 4 18 ounces canned sweet potatoes -- drained and chopped
- 14 1/2 ounces canned tomato wedges -- undrained
- 1 1/2 cups tomato juice
- 3/4 cup apple juice
- 1 teaspoon ginger root --up to 2, grated
- 2 cups green beans, frozen -- cut crosswise
  1/3 cup peanut butter
  6 cups cooked brown rice

Heat the oil in a large skillet over medium-high heat. Cook Beef, Add the cabbage and garlic; cook, stirring, until the cabbage is tender-crisp, about 5 minutes. Stir in the sweet potatoes, tomatoes, tomato juice, apple juice, ginger. Reduce the heat to medium-low; cover. Simmer until hot and bubbling, about 6 minutes.
Stir in the green beans and simmer, uncovered, for 5 minutes.Stir in the peanut butter until well-blended and hot, about 1 minute. Spoon over rice.

*Note: Low Fat, or use chicken, lamb, fish. Liver can be usedas well.

Divine Doggy Dinner

- 1/2 pound ground beef -- or turkey, chicken, lamb
- 1/4 cup cooked rice
- 1 small potato
- 1/4 cup green beans -- about 5-8 beans
- 1/4 teaspoon garlic powder

Brown the meat in a pan. When completely cooked, drain the fat. Add the cooked rice; mix well. Set aside. Cut the potato and beans into small bite-sized pieces. Place in a pot with water; bring to a boil. Simmer until veggies are tender (about 15-20 minutes). Drain. Add the vegetables to the meat mixture. Add garlic powder; toss thoroughly under low heat. Let the dinner cool thoroughly before serving to prevent burning.
Yield: about 2 dinners

Dog Powder Mix

- 1 cup brewer's yeast
- 1 cup bone meal
- 1/2 cup kelp powder
- 1/2 cup alfalfa powder

Mix well add to air-tight container. Keep in freezer if desiredadd one tablespoon to dogs food each day.

Doggie Quiche

- 4 whole egg
- 1 tablespoon cream
- 2/3 cup milk, skim
- 3 ounces meat --*see Note
- 2 ounces shredded lowfat cheddar cheese -- or other type
- 1 whole pie crust (9 inch)
- 1/2 teaspoon garlic powder --optional
- 1 sprig parsley -- chopped fine

Pre-heat oven to 375F degrees.
Wisk egg, cream, milk together, then pour into pie crust. Add meat, cheese evenly Bake for 30-45 min. Till done. Let it cool.
Sprinkle fresh parsley.
Note: fine chopped, any type of meat they like. Pre cooked, unless you use liver.
Fresh shredded veggies can be used as well.

Ellie's Dog Loaf

- 2 1/8 cups water
- 2 cups brown rice
- 2 large potatoes
- 2 large carrots
- 1 1/8 pounds pumpkin
- 1 large onion
- 2 cloves garlic
- 3/4 bunch silver beet
- 1 cup whole meal pasta --or Soya pasta
- 2 cups rolled oats
- 1 cup whole meal flour
- 1 1/8 pounds mince (or liver or fish)
- 3 eggs

Boil the rice in water for 10 - 15 minutes and chop the veggies (I put them through the food processor) Add the veggies and pasta to the rice and cook for 10 minutes. Turn off the heat and leave to cool (not vital if you're like me and in a rush!) Add mince, eggs, herbs, rolled oats and flour and mix together. Add more oats or flour if mixture is sticky (should be like a fruit cake mix)

Spoon into oiled and floured loaf tins and bake in a hot oven 180 degrees CENTIGRADE for 1 hour.

Remove from tins ,turn oven off and return loaves to oven for 5 - 10 minutes to firm bottom crust.

Take out of oven, leave to cool and use immediately or wrap in foil and freeze.

Makes about 3 - 4 loaves.

Fido's Cheese Nuggets

- 1 cup Oatmeal --uncooked
- 1 1/2 cups Hot Water --or Meat Juices
- 4 oz Grated Cheese --one cup
- 1 Egg --beaten
- 1 cup Wheat Germ
- 1/4 cup Margarine
- 1/2 cup Powdered Milk
- 1/4 teaspoon Salt
- 1 cup Cornmeal
- 3 cups Whole Wheat Flour

In large bowl pour hot water over oatmeal and margarine: letstand for 5 minutes. Stir in powdered milk, grated cheese, salt and egg. Add cornmeal andwheat germ. Mix well. Add flour, 1/3 cup at a time, mixing well after each addition.Knead 3 or 4 minutes, adding more flour if necessary to make a very stiff dough. Patorroll dough to 1/2 inch thickness. Cut into bone shaped biscuits and place on a greasedbaking sheet. Bake for 1 hour at 300 degrees. Turn off heat and leave in oven for 1 1/2hours or longer. Makes approximately 2 1/4 pounds.

Goulash

- 1 pound ground beef -- *see Note
- 2 cups cooked brown rice
- 2 cans vegetables --*see Note
- 2 whole egg -- *see Note
- 1 can mackerel, canned
- 2 cloves garlic --minced
- 1 pound chicken liver -- or gizzards

Pulverize veggies, either in a blender, processor, grinder, etc. Mix all ingredients together in a big pot. Add enough water to cover, mix well. if you feed raw, which we do, place into containers, enough for one feeding in each, and freeze. We use plastic baggies. If you don't feed raw, cover the pot and simmer for about 2 hrs, stirring occasionally. When it is done cooking, cool, and place into containers or baggies, enough for one feeding in each and freeze. Simply get out in the morning to thaw in the fridge.

Note: ground beef, ground turkey, ground venison, etc.

Note: fresh veggies (about 3 cups)- broccoli, asparagus, sweet potatoes, green beans, carrots, spinach, kale. CUT UP.

Note: shells crushed and added

Dogs get this every evening for dinner, with 1/4-1/2c kibble mixed in, depending on size of dog. feed 1cup per 15 lbs body weight.

Greyhound Green Bean Grub

- 1 pound green beans -- fresh or frozen, sliced
- 1 can cream of mushroom soup
- 1/2 cup milk
- 1/2 cup cheddar cheese --plus extra

Mix all ingredients together except beans. Place beans in ovencasserole, add sauce mixture and stir well. Cover and bake in a 350 degree oven for25 minutes. Uncover the casserole and sprinkle top with more cheddar cheese. Bake 5minutes more. Let cool. *This is great as an occasional treat with regular kibble - plushumans can share also!

Hors D'ogs

- 1/4 cup cheddar cheese – grated
- 2 tablespoons safflower oil
- 1/2 cup rice krispies®
- 1/2 teaspoon minced garlic
- 1/4 cup swiss cheese -- grated

Combine cheeses, garlic and oil. Using plastic wrap, shape mixture into a log about 1 inch in diameter and 8 inches long. Roll log in Rice Krispies.Refrigerate. Slice into half-inch rounds and serve.

Labrador Loaf

- 1 cup Amaranth
- 1 cup Dates --dried
- 1 cup boiling water -- or beef broth
- 2 cups whole wheat flour
- 2 teaspoons baking powder --non aluminum sulfate
- 2 tablespoons canola oil
- 4 ounces Egg Beaters ® 99% egg substitute
- 2 cups beef broth
- 1/2 pound ground beef, extra lean

Put Amaranth and Dates in a bowl, pour boiling water over and allow to soak 30 minutes. Pre-heat oven to 350.
In a large bowl, mix egg beaters and canola oil and beef broth and beef, mix well. Add whole wheat flour and baking soda, and the soaked Amaranth and Dates. Mix well.
Pour into an oiled loaf pan, bake for 1 hour or till done.
*Note: Use Vegetable Broth and 1/2 Pound of Textured Vegetable Protein for a Vegetarian Diet

Lhasa Apso Lamb

- 1 pound lamb, ground --cooked
- 2 cups cooked brown rice
- 2 cups cooked white rice
- 1 cup yogurt, skim milk
- 4 cloves garlic --crushed
- 1/4 cup green beans, frozen -- chopped
- 1/4 cup carrots, frozen --chopped
- 1/4 cup kale, frozen --chopped

Cook Lamb and drain off excess fat if desired. Defrost frozen veggies, but don't cook them and chop to desired size.

In a large bowl mix cooked lamb, cooked rice, chopped vegetables, garlic and yogurt. Slightly heat if desired to serve.

Refrigerate or freeze portions in zip lock bags. Should yield 3to 6 servings.

Meat and Grain Menu

- 2 cups brown rice -- cooked
- 2/3 cup meat --lean
- 2 teaspoons lard -- or veggie oil
- 1/4 cup Vegetables --grated, no onion
- *Supplements

Mix the above. You can cook the meat if you want to, use your judgment. Serve slightly warm.

*For supplements, add 2 tsp. powder and 1 tsp. oil to feed daily- this is for a 5-15 lb. dog, and the book instructs to use double supplements for a puppy.

Meatball Mania

- 1/2 pound ground beef
- 2 tablespoons grated cheese
- 1 carrot -- finely grated
- 1/2 teaspoon garlic powder
- 1/2 cup bread crumbs --w/w is best
- 1 egg -- beaten
- 1/2 tablespoon tomato paste

Preheat oven to 350 degrees. Combine all ingredients together; mix thoroughly. Roll into meatballs - whatever size is appropriate for your dog.

Place on a cookie sheet sprayed with non-fat cooking spray. Bake for 15-20 minutes, or until they are brown and firm.

Cool and store in the fridge or freezer.

MuttLoaf

- 1/2 cup amaranth --*see Note
- 1 1/2 cups chicken broth
- 1 1/2 pounds ground chicken -- or turkey
- 1/2 cup cottage cheese
- 2 whole egg
- 1/2 cup oats, rolled (raw)
- 1/4 cup carrot --finely chopped
- 1/4 cup spinach --finely chopped
- 1/4 cup zucchini --finely chopped
- 2 cloves garlic
- 1 tablespoon olive oil

Add amaranth and chicken broth to sauce pan and bring to a boil, reduce heat and simmer for 20 minutes. Set aside and let cool.

Preheat oven to 350.

In a large mixing bowl add meat, cottage cheese, veggies, and eggs. Mix thoroughly. Add wheat germ, cooled amaranth and olive oil mix well.

Add mixture to loaf pan, bake at 350 for 1 hour or until done.

Note: Amaranth can be found in a health food store, if not use barley. Barley will need 4 cups of broth and 50 minutes to cook.

Mutt's favorite rice n' hamburger

- 2 cups rice
- 1/2 pound hamburger meat
- 1 teaspoon vegetable oil
- 1 clove garlic
- 1/2 cup carrots or broccoli or spinach
- 4 cups water

Put all ingredients into a large pot, boil until done, then cool off and serve. I feed my

dogs this kind of meal or a variation every day, instead of store-bought food. They've got shiny coats, are full of energy and love eating dinner again!

Muttzoh Balls

- 1 cup natural dry dog food
- 2 Eggs --beaten lightly
- 1 teaspoon cod liver oil
- 1/3 cup Cold water
- 2 dashes garlic powder
- 1/2 cup cream of chicken soup, condensed

Grind dry dog food smooth in a food processor or blender. Lightly beat egg and add oil.

Mix all moist ingredients together except soup. Add to dry ingredients. Form into 1/2" balls. In large pan, bring 1 quart water to boiling to which youhave added 1/2 cup chicken soup or the 2 bouillon cubes. Drop balls into boilingwater. Boil for 3 minutes. Remove from water, drain and cool. Refrigerate

---

Poodle Pasta

- 3 1/2 cups whole wheat flour
- 8 ounces beef liver
- 3 whole egg
- 1 tablespoon olive oil
- 8 tablespoons butter --optional

Puree beef liver in blender until smooth. Add eggs and blend for about a minute.

Put flour in a large mixing bowl and make a well in the center of the flour.
Pour liver and egg mixture into well along with olive oil. Mix well until thoroughly combined.

Turn dough out on floured board and knead well for at least 5 minutes or until smooth and shiny.

Wrap dough in plastic wrap and let dough rest in refrigerator for at least 1 hour, no longer than 2 days.

When ready to make pasta, divide dough into 8 equal portions, approximately 4 oz. each.

Form into desired pasta shapes with hands or use pasta machine.

Cook in rapidly boiling water until al dente. For thin noodles, approximately 10 minutes, for thicker noodles a few minutes longer.

Drain noodles and toss with 1 tablespoon butter per serving, if desired.

Instead of butter, try tossing noodles with 1 tablespoon olive oil, canola oil or other oil high in omega-3 and omega-6 fatty acids.

Yield: "2 pounds"

Serving Ideas : Toss cooked pasta with finely shredded fresh vegetables such as carrots, zucchini, broccoli, sweet potatoes, etc. before serving. Mix cooked pasta with 2 tablespoons low-fat cottage cheese and/or yogurt per serving fora smooth, creamy sauce.

Potatoes Au Canine Or Feline

- 3 cups boiled potatoes -- sliced
- 2 tablespoons vegetables --grated
- 1/2 cup Creamed cottage cheese
- 1 tablespoon Nutritional Yeast
- 2 tablespoons Grated carrots
- 1/4 cup Whole milk
- 1/4 cup Grated cheese

Layer in a casserole dish the first 5 ingredients. Then pour the milk on top of all; sprinkle with cheese. Bake about 15 minutes at 350 until cheese melts and slightly browns. Serve cool.

Notes: As a potato substitute, you can use 3 cups of cooked oatmeal or 3 cups cooked brown rice.

Ravioli Woofer Stuffing

- 3 tablespoons whole wheat flour
- 3/4 cup cottage cheese, 2% fat
- 2 eggs
- 1/2 cup cooked Atlantic salmon --finely diced
- 2 tablespoons parsley sprig --finely chopped

Prepare the PoodleRice and Meat Dinner

- 1 cup meat --*see Note 4 cups rice
- 1 cup vegetables --*see Note
- 1 tablespoon vegetable oil
- 2 cloves garlic

Boil all ingredients together in a large pot. Be sure that pork is cooked all the way through. Cool food off and serve.

Note: choose one: hamburger, ground pork (cook all the way through), ground chicken, ground turkey, or liver

Note: choose one or more of these: sweet potato, regular potato, green beans, carrots, spinach

For Variety: Noodles and Meat Same ingredients as RiceandMeatDinner, except for this: Boil 1 pound noodles separately. Mix noodles in withmeatandvegetable mixture when ready to serve. Italian and Chinese noodles will bothwork.

Try to substitute mackerel (a fish) for meat in some meals.Iusuallybuy the canned stuff which has little bones in it. They can eat these bones. A littleofthecanned stuff goes a long way though--it has a lot of salt!

Rice Flour Dog Cookie

- 1 1/2 cups white rice flour
- 1 1/4 cups grated cheddar cheese
- 1/4 pound safflower oil -- margarine 1 clove garlic --crushed

Grate the cheese and let stand until it reaches room temperature. Cream the cheese with the softened margarine, garlic, and flour. Add enough milktoform into a ball. Chill for 1/2 hour. Roll onto floured board. Cut into shapes and bakeat375 for 15 minutes or until slightly brown, and firm. Makes 2 to 3 dozen, depending onsize.

Shih Tzu Sushi

- 1 can salmon, canned, pink -- reserve liquid
- 1 cup brown rice
- 2 cups water -- plus salmon liquid
- 1 whole egg, hard-boiled -- chopped
- 1/2 cup peas and carrots, frozen -- or more if desired
- 1 tablespoon fresh parsley -- chopped
- 2 tablespoons cod liver oil
- 1 package Nori Sheets -- *see Note

Drain salmon, reserve liquid for rice. do not remove bones or skin, flake with fork.

Defrost peas and carrots.

In a sauce pan add salmon liquid, water, brown rice, cook. let cool to touch.

In a mixing bowl add salmon, brown rice, chopped egg, peas and carrots, and parsley, cod liver oil. Mix well.

place one nori sheet on a flat surface and spread mixture 1/4 inch over nori, leave 1/4 inch edge of nori and dampen with water. And roll. repeat till nori sheets are used, or mixture is gone.

Individually wrap in plastic wrap, refrigerate till ready to serve.

Cut rolls into size for your doggie.

Note: Nori Sheets is dried seaweed found in the oriental sectionof your grocery store or specialty shop. This recipe freezes well also.

Trail Dog Grub

- 2 Cups Amaranth -- Cooked
- 1 Cup Lentils, Cooked
- 1 Cup Vegetables -- *See Note
- 2 Tablespoons Cod Liver Oil
- 1 Pound Buffalo
- 1 Cup Beef Broth

Cut Buffalo meat to size for your dog, add to Stock Pot along with beef broth, vegetables and cod liver oil, cook 10 minutes. Add Water if more moisture is needed during cooking.

Add cooked amaranth, cooked lentils mix well. Allow to cooland serve.

*Note: Chopped to size for your dog, Assorted Veggies, carrot,kale, sweet potato, asparagus, zucchini etc.

Veggie Vittles

- 1 egg -- beaten
- 1/3 cup applesauce
- 1 cup vegetables --*see Note
- 1 cup cooked rice
- 1 tablespoon brewer's yeast

Mix all ingredients well. Drop by rounded teaspoonfuls onto a greased cookie sheet.

Bake in a preheated 350 degree oven for about 12 minutes, or until lightly browned and firm. Cool. Store in the fridge, or freeze.
Note: mashed or grated small. Any desired veggies can be used,such as zucchini, peas, carrots, potatoes, etc...

Vizsla Stew

- 2 cups barley
- 1/2 cup wild rice
- 9 cups chicken broth
- 4 cups rabbits -- boned, *See Note
- 1/2 cup kale -- chopped fine
- 1/2 cup asparagus -- chopped fine
- 1/2 cup lima beans -- chopped fine
- 1/2 cup carrots -- chopped fine
- 1 cup potato -- chopped fine
- 4 cloves garlic -- chopped fine
- 1/3 cup canola oil
- 1 cup yogurt, skim milk

In a large pot, place the bones and chicken broth. Bring to a rapid boil.

Add the long cooking Wild Rice and Barley, reduce heat to a simmer and cover. After 20 minutes and the rabbit, cook another 30 minutes.

Wash and chop the vegetables, place in a mixing bowl, add canola oil and yogurt, mix.

Allow Barley and Wild Rice to cool. Remove bones. Drain liquid if needed. Pour into the mixing bowl and mix well.

Refrigerate or freeze leftovers in portions in separate containers.

*Note: 2 rabbits, 4 to 6 pounds, bone the rabbit and cube to the size for your dog. Add the bones to the chicken broth.

Note: frozen vegetables may be used, run under cold water todefrost.

Weimaraner Walleye

- 3 pounds walleye pike fillets
- 2 ounces chicken livers -- diced fine
- 2 cups fish stock
- 3 cups cooked brown rice
- 1/4 cup cooked wild rice
- 1/4 cup kale, frozen
- 1/2 cup green beans, frozen
- 1/4 cup collard greens, frozen
- 1/4 cup corn, frozen
- 1/4 cup potatoes, frozen
- 1 tablespoon cod liver oil

pre heat oven to 350.
In a baking dish add walleye fillets diced chicken livers, pour in fish stock and cod liver oil, add frozen veggies, cover and bake 20 to 30 minutes or till done.
In a large bowl add cooked rice, and the juices from the baking dish along with the cooked veggies, mix well. chunk the walleye into a size for your dog and mix well, if needed chop vegetables to a size for your dog.
Allow to cool and serve. freeze leftovers or keep in fridge covered.

THE ULTIMATE GUIDE TO

PET CARE

EVERYTHING YOU NEED TO KNOW TO KEEP
YOUR PET HAPPY AND HEALTHY

CONTENTS

CHAPTER 1

CHOOSING THE RIGHT PET

Choosing the Right Pet

Petsprovide us with companionship, love, andasenseof responsibility. However, choosingthe right petcan bea dauntingtask. Here are some factors to consider when making your decision.

The benefits of having a pet:

- Pets can reduce stress and anxiety

- They provide companionship and can help alleviate loneliness

- Owning a pet can improve physical health through increased exercise

- Pets can teach responsibility and empathy

- They can enhance social interactions and provide opportunities for socialisation

Your lifestyle:

Consider how much time you have to dedicate to a pet. Some pets require more attention and exercise than others. If you work long hours, a low-maintenance pet may be a better fit.

Your living space:

If youlive in a small apartment, a large dog may not be practical. Consider the size of your home and whether you have a yard or outdoor space.

Your budget:

Owning a petcan be expensive. Consider the cost of food, toys, grooming, and veterinary care before making your decision.

Your family:

Ifyouhavechildren or other pets, consider whether the pet you choose will be a good fit for your family dynamic.

Different types of pets and their characteristics:

DOGS

Dogs are loyal, loving, and make great companions. They require daily exercise and training, but can provide a lot of joy and love in return.

CATS

Catsare independent, low-maintenance pets that can be affectionate and playful. They are often a good choice for those with busy lifestyles.

BIRDS

Birds are intelligent, social pets that can be very entertaining. They require a lot of attention and care, including daily cleaning of their cage and feeding.

Different types of pets and their characteristics:

FISH

Fish are low-maintenance pets that can be relaxing to watch. They require a properly-sized tank, clean water, and appropriate food.

REPTILES

Reptiles can make great pets for those who are interested in exotic animals. They require specific environmental conditions and specialized diets.

SMALL ANIMALS

Small animals such as rabbits, guinea pigs, and hamsters can make great pets for children. They are low-maintenance, but require daily attention and care.

CONCLUSION

In conclusion, choosing the right pet requires careful consideration of your lifestyle, living space, budget, and family. By selecting the right pet for your individual needs, you can enjoy a fulfilling and rewarding relationship with your furry friend.

CHAPTER 2

NUTRITION AND FEEDING

Nutrition and Feeding

Propernutritionis essential foryourpet'shealthand well-being.Hereare someimportantfactorstoconsider when feeding yourpet.

The importance of nutrition in pet health:

- Nutrition affects all aspects of your pet's health, including their coat, skin, immune system, and organ function.

- A balanced diet can prevent health problems and prolong your pet's life.

- Different pets have different nutritional needs, depending on their age, breed, size, and activity level.

Dry food:

Dry foodis a convenient and affordable option. Look for high-quality ingredients, including protein, fats, and fibre. Avoid foods that contain fillers and artificial preservatives.

Wet food:

Wetfood provides more moisture and can be more palatable for some pets. Look for wet food that contains high-quality protein and vegetables.

Raw food:

Rawfood diets are becoming more popular, but can be risky if not prepared properly. Consult with your veterinarian before choosing a raw food diet.

Homemade food:

Homemade diets can be healthy if they are well-balanced and include all necessary nutrients. Consult with a veterinary nutritionist before feeding your pet homemade food.

Feeding schedules and portion control:

- Follow the feeding guidelines on the food package or as recommended by your veterinarian.

- Divide your pet's daily food intake into two or more meals to prevent overeating.

- Avoid free-feeding, where food is available at all times, as this can lead to obesity.

Treats and snacks:

- Treats should make up no more than 10% of your pet's daily diet.

- Choose treats that are made with high-quality ingredients and are appropriate for your pet's size and health needs.

- Avoid giving your pet table scraps, as they can be high in fat and salt.

CONCLUSION

In conclusion:

In conclusion, proper nutrition is crucial to your pet's health and longevity. By choosing high-quality food, following a feeding schedule, and controlling portions, you can ensure your pet is getting the nutrients they need. Treats should be given sparingly, and should not make up a significant portion of your pet's diet. Consult with your veterinarian if you have any questions or concerns about your pet's nutrition.

CHAPTER 3

EXERCISE AND
PLAYTIME

Exercise and Playtime

Exercise andplaytime areimportantforkeeping your pet healthy, happy, and mentally stimulated.Here's what you needto know about exercise andplaytimefor your pet.

The benefits of exercise for pets:

- Exercise can help prevent obesity, diabetes, and other health problems.

- Regular exercise can reduce stress and anxiety in pets.

- Exercise provides an opportunity for socialisation and can strengthen the bond between you and your pet.

- Physical activity can improve your pet's overall behaviour and obedience.

DOGS

DOGS

Weight management:
Regular exercise helpsdogs maintain a healthy weight, reducing the risk of obesity and associated health problems.

Improved cardiovascular health:
Exercise canimprove dogs' heart health by strengthening the heart and improving blood circulation.

Better joint health:
Exercise can help keep dogs' joints limber and improve range of motion, reducing the risk of arthritis and other joint problems.

Improved behaviour:
Dogs whoget enough exercise are often calmer and less likely to exhibit destructive or problematic behaviours.

CATS

Types of exercise and activities for different pets:

CATS

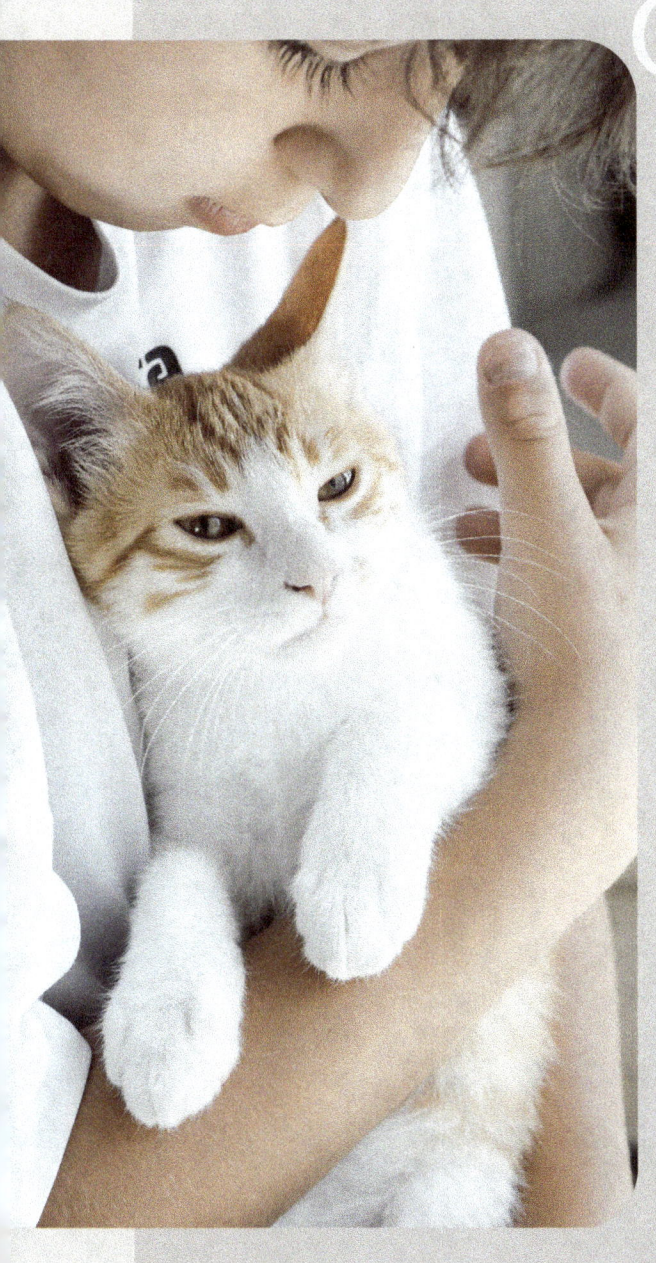

Weight management:
Exercise canhelp catsmaintain a healthy weight and reduce the risk of obesity and associated health problems.

Improved cardiovascular health:
Exercisecanimprove cats' heart health and reduce the risk of heart disease.

Better joint health:
Exercise can help keep cats' joints limber and reduce the risk of arthritis and other joint problems.

Improved behaviour:
Cats whoget enough exercise are often calmer and less likely to exhibit destructive or problematic behaviours.

RABBITS

RABBITS

Weight management:
Exercise can help rabbits maintain a healthy weight and reduce the risk of obesity and associated health problems.

Improved cardiovascular health:
Exercisecan improverabbits' heart health and reduce the risk of heart disease.

Better joint health:
Regular exercise can help keep rabbits' digestive system functioning properly and reduce the risk of digestive problems.

Mental stimulation:
Exercisecan provide mental stimulation for rabbits, keeping them mentally sharp and engaged.

GUINEA PIGS

Guinea pigs

Weight management:
Exercise can help guinea pigs maintain a healthy weight and reduce the risk of obesity and associated health problems.

Improved cardiovascular health:
Exercisecan improveguinea pigs' heart health and reduce the risk of heart disease.

Better digestive health:
Regular exercisecan help keep guinea pigs' digestive system functioning properly and reduce the risk of digestive problems.

Mental stimulation:
Exercise can provide mental stimulation for guinea pigs, keeping them mentally sharp and engaged.

HAMSTERS

Hamsters

Weight management:
Exercise can help hamsters maintain a healthy weight and reduce the risk of obesity and associated health problems.

Improved cardiovascular health:
Exercisecan improvehamsters' heart health and reduce the risk of heart disease.

Improved mood:
Exercise canhelpimprove hamsters' mood and reduce stress and anxiety.

Mental stimulation:
Exercisecan provide mental stimulation for hamsters, keeping them mentally sharp and engaged.

How to create a safe and stimulating play environment:

1. Remove any hazards, such as toxic plants and wires, from your pet's play area.

2. Provide your pet with toys that are safe and appropriate for their age and size.

3. Rotate your pet's toys regularly to prevent boredom.

4. Supervise your pet during playtime and avoid rough play or aggressive behaviour.

5. Create a comfortable and inviting space for your pet to play, with access to food, water, and a place to rest.

CONCLUSION

In conclusion:

In conclusion, regular exercise and playtime are essential for your pet's physical and mental health. Different pets have different exercise needs and preferences, so tailor your playtime to suit their individual needs. Create a safe and stimulating environment for your pet to play in, and supervise them during playtime to prevent injury. By incorporating regular exercise and playtime into your pet's routine, you can ensure they lead a happy and healthy life.

GROOMING AND HYGIENE

Grooming and Hygiene

Propergroomingand hygieneareimportantforyourpet's
healthandwell-being.Here's what youneedtoknow
about grooming your pet.

The importance of grooming for pet health:

- Grooming can prevent skin infections, matting, and parasites.

- Regular grooming can reduce shedding and minimise allergies.

- Grooming provides an opportunity for you to check your pet's overall health, including their eyes, ears, and teeth.

- Proper grooming can improve your pet's appearance and comfort.

DOGS

for different pets:

DOGS

Brushing:
Brush your dog's coat regularly to prevent matting and tangling. The frequency of brushing depends on the dog's coat type.

Bathing:
Bathe your dog every 6 to 8 weeks or as needed. Use a dog-specific shampoo and conditioner to avoid skin irritation.

Nail trimming:
Trim your dog's nails every 3 to 4 weeks to prevent overgrowth, which can cause discomfort and potential injury.

Teeth brushing:
Brush your dog's teeth at least twice a week to prevent dental issues.

CATS

CATS

Brushing:
Brush your cat's coat regularly to remove loose fur and prevent hairballs.

Bathing:
Most cats do not need regular baths unless they have a skin condition or get into something messy.

Nail trimming:
Trimyour cat'snails every 4 to 6 weeks to prevent overgrowth and potential scratching of furniture or people.

Teeth brushing:
Brush yourcat's teeth at least twice a week to prevent dental issues.

RABBITS

Different grooming techniques for different pets:

RABBITS

Brushing:
Brush your rabbit's coat regularly to remove loose fur and prevent matting.

Bathing:
Rabbitsshould not be bathed unless they have a skin condition that requires it. Spot cleaning with a damp cloth can be done as needed.

Nail trimming:
Trimyour rabbit's nails every 6 to 8 weeks to prevent overgrowth.

Teeth brushing:
Rabbits' teeth grow continuously, so they need regular dental checkups and teeth filing as needed.

GUINEA PIGS

for different pets:

Guinea pigs

Brushing:
Brush your guinea pig's coat regularly to remove loose fur and prevent matting.

Bathing:
Guinea pigs should be bathed every 4 to 6 weeks using a guinea pig-specific shampoo and conditioner.

Nail trimming:
Trim yourguineapig's nails every 4 to 6 weeks to prevent overgrowth.

Teeth brushing:
Like rabbits,guinea pigs' teeth grow continuously, so they need regular dental checkups and teeth filing as needed.

HAMSTERS

Different grooming techniques for different pets:

Hamsters

Brushing:
Hamsters do not require brushing.

Bathing:
Hamsters should not be bathed unless they have a skin condition that requires it. Spot cleaning with a damp cloth can be done as needed.

Nail trimming:
Hamsters' nails usually wear down naturally, but if they get too long, they can be trimmed carefully.

Teeth brushing:
Hamsters' teeth also grow continuously, so they need to chew on hard objects to keep them trimmed. If their teeth become overgrown, they need veterinary attention.

CONCLUSION

In conclusion, proper grooming and hygiene are essential for your pet's health and comfort. Different pets require different grooming techniques, so tailor your grooming routine to suit your pet's needs. Regular bathing, brushing, and nail trimming can help prevent skin infections, matting, and overgrowth. Dental hygiene is also important for preventing tooth decay and gum disease. By incorporating regular grooming and hygiene into your pet's routine, you can ensure they lead a happy and healthy life.

CHAPTER 5

TRAINING AND BEHAVIOURAL ISSUES

Training and Behavioral Issues

Training your pet is an essential part of being a responsible pet owner. Here's what you need to know about training and addressing behavioural issues in pets.

The benefits of training for pets and their owners:

- Training helps establish a bond between you and your pet and promotes good behaviour.

- Proper training can prevent problem behaviours and help your pet become a well-adjusted member of your household.

- Training can be fun and rewarding for both you and your pet.

Basic obedience training:

- Basic obedience training includes teaching your pet commands such as sit, stay, come, and heel.

- Start with simple commands and reward your pet for good behaviour.

- Consistency is key, so be patient and repeat commands regularly.

- Use positive reinforcement, such as treats or praise, to encourage good behaviour.

Addressing common behavioural issues:

- **Barking:** Excessive barking can be caused by boredom, anxiety, or fear. Address the root cause of the behaviour and provide your pet with toys, exercise, and attention.

- **Chewing:** Chewing is a natural behaviour for pets but can become a problem if your pet chews on furniture or shoes. Provide your pet with appropriate chew toys and praise them for using them.

- **Jumping:** Jumping is a common problem for dogs and can be caused by excitement or a desire for attention. Teach your pet the "off" command and reward them for good behaviour.

Socialisation and interaction with other pets:

- Socialisation is the process of introducing your pet to new people, animals, and environments.

- Proper socialisation can prevent fear and aggression and help your pet become well-adjusted and confident.

- Start socialising your pet at a young age and expose them to a variety of situations and environments.

DOGS

COMMON TRAINING AND BEHAVIOURAL ISSUES FOR DOGS

Pottytraining:
Dogs need to be trained to go outside or use a designated indoor area for elimination.

Barking:
Dogs may bark excessively, which can be a nuisance to neighbours and other pets.

Leash pulling:
Dogs may pull onthe leash during walks, making it difficult to control them.

Obsessive behaviours:
Dogs may exhibit obsessive behaviours, such as compulsive licking or chasing their tail, which can be a sign of anxiety or boredom.

Stealing food or objects:
Dogs may steal foodor objects, which can be a nuisance or even dangerous if they ingest something harmful.

Aggression:
Some dogs may exhibit aggressive behaviour towards people or other animals.

Jumping on people:
Dogs may jump onpeople as a way of greeting, which can be dangerous or uncomfortable.

Fearfulness:
Some dogs may be shy or fearful, and need to be socialised and trained to be more comfortable around people and other animals.

Separation anxiety:
Somedogs maybecome anxious or destructive when left alone.

Destructive chewing:
Dogs may chew onfurniture, shoes, or other objects, causing damage.

CATS

Scratching:
Cats need to be trained to use a scratching post or other designated area for scratching.

Litter box training:
Catsneed to betrained to use a litter box for elimination.

Inactivity:
Somecats may become sedentary or inactive if they do not get enough exercise or stimulation.

Destructive behaviour:
Cats mayscratch furnitureor other objects, knock things over, or climb on surfaces where they are not allowed.

Fearfulness:
Some cats may be shy or fearful, and need to be socialised and trained to be more comfortable around people and other animals.

Over-grooming:
Some cats may excessively groom themselves, leading to hair loss or skin irritation.

Meowing excessively:
Some cats maymeow excessively, which can be a sign of stress, anxiety, or a medical issue.

Begging for food:
Cats may beg forfood or steal food from counters or tables.

Inappropriate urination:
Some cats may urinate outside of the litter box, which can be a sign of stress or a medical issue.

Aggression:
Somecats may exhibit aggressive behaviour towards people or other animals.

RABBITS

COMMON TRAINING AND BEHAVIOURAL ISSUES FOR RABBITS

Chewing:
Rabbits need to be trained to chew on appropriate objects and not on furniture or other items.

Litter box training:

Rabbits can betrainedto use a litter box for elimination.

Fearfulness:
Some rabbits may be shy or fearful, and need to be socialised and trained to be more comfortable around people and other animals.

Destructive behaviour:

Rabbitsmay chew on wiresor other objects that can be dangerous or damaging.

Digging:
Rabbits are natural diggers and may dig up carpet or other flooring, or dig holes in the yard if allowed to roam outside.

Over-grooming:
Some rabbitsmay excessively groom themselves, leading to hair loss or skin irritation.

Obesity:
Rabbits can become overweight if they do not get enough exercise or are fed a diet that is too high in calories.

Aggression towards other rabbits:
Ifmultiple rabbits are kept together, they may exhibit aggressive behaviour towards each other.

Lethargy:
Somerabbits may become lethargic or inactive if they do not get enough exercise or stimulation.

GUINEA PIGS

COMMON TRAINING AND BEHAVIOURAL ISSUES FOR GUINEA PIGS

Chewing:
Guinea pigs need to be trained to chew on appropriate objects and not on furniture or other items.

Litter box training:
Guineapigs can be trained to use a litter box for elimination.

Obesity:
Guinea pigs can become overweight if they do not get enough exercise or are fed a diet that is too high in calories.

Destructive behaviour:
Guinea pigs may chewon wires or other objects that can be dangerous or damaging.

Fearfulness:
Someguinea pigs may be shy or fearful, and need to be socialised and trained to be more comfortable around people and other animals.

Aggression towards other guinea pigs:
Ifmultipleguinea pigsare kept together, they may exhibit aggressive behaviour towards each other.

Inactivity:
Some guinea pigs may become sedentary or inactive if they do not get enough exercise or stimulation.

Overgrown teeth:
Guinea pigsneedtochew on hay and other roughage to keep their teeth from overgrowing, otherwise it can lead to dental issues.

Respiratory issues:
Guinea pigs are susceptible to respiratory infections if kept in a poorly ventilated or dirty environment.

REPTILES

Handling:
Some reptiles may become stressed or agitated when handled, and need to be trained to be more comfortable with being picked up and handled.

Feeding:
Some reptiles may be picky eaters or may not eat enough, which can lead to health issues.

Environmental issues:
Reptiles require specific temperature and humidity levels, and may exhibit behavioural issues if their environment is not properly maintained.

Shedding:
Reptiles need to shed their skin periodically, and may require assistance or treatment if they are having difficulty shedding.

Aggression:
Some reptiles may exhibit aggressive behaviour towards people or other animals.

Territorial behavior:
Some reptiles may exhibit territorial behaviour towards other reptiles, which can lead to aggression or fighting.

Biting:
Some reptiles may bite if they feel threatened or are handled improperly.

Escape attempts:
Some reptiles may attempt to escape their enclosure, which can be dangerous for both the reptile and any people or animals nearby.

Aggression towards prey:

Some reptiles may exhibit aggressive behaviour towards their prey, which can lead to feeding issues or injuries.

HAMSTERS

Biting:
Somehamsters may bite if they feel threatened or are handled improperly.

Escaping:
Hamsters are good at escaping their enclosure and can be difficult to catch if they get loose.

Litter box training:
Some hamsters can be trained to use a litter box, but it may take time and patience.

Destructive behaviour:
Hamsters may chew on items in their cage, such as toys or bedding, which can be damaging.

Fearfulness:
Some hamsters may be shy or fearful, and need to be socialised and trained to be more comfortable around people.

Aggression towards other hamsters:
Ifmultiple hamsters arekept together, they may exhibit aggressive behaviour towards each other.

Obesity:
Hamsters can become overweight if they do not get enough exercise or are fed a diet that is too high in calories.

Inactivity:
Some hamsters may become sedentary or inactive if they do not get enough exercise or stimulation.

Sleeping during the day:
Hamsters are nocturnal animals and may sleep during the day, which can make it difficult to interact with them.

CONCLUSION

In conclusion, training and addressing behavioural issues in pets is an essential part of being a responsible pet owner. Basic obedience training can help prevent problem behaviours and establish a strong bond between you and your pet. Addressing common behavioural issues, such as barking, chewing, and jumping, requires patience and consistency. Socialisation is also important for preventing fear and aggression and helping your pet become well-adjusted and confident. By incorporating training and addressing behavioural issues into your pet's routine, you can ensure they lead a happy and healthy life.

HEALTH CARE AND VETERINARY VISITS

Health Care and Veterinary Visits

Your pet's health is essential to their overall well-being. Here's what you need to know about health care and veterinary visits.

The importance of regular checkups and preventive care:

- Regular checkups and preventive care are essential for maintaining your pet's health.

- Schedule annual checkups with your veterinarian, and keep your pet up-to-date on vaccinations and preventive treatments.

- Preventive care can include flea and tick prevention, heart worm prevention, and dental care.

Obesity:
Obesityis a growing concern among pets, especially dogs and cats. Signs of obesity include difficulty breathing, lethargy, and a reluctance to exercise.

Dental problems:
Bad breath,red or swollen gums, and tartar buildup are some signs of dental problems in pets.

Skin allergies:
Common signsofskin allergies in pets include itching, excessive scratching, hair loss, and skin irritation.

Arthritis:
Arthritis is common in older pets, and signs of arthritis include difficulty standing up, limping, and a reluctance to move.

Common health issues and how to recognise them:

Diabetes:
Diabetes is becoming increasingly common in pets, especially in overweight animals. Signs of diabetes include increased thirst and urination, weight loss, and a lack of energy.

Urinary tract infections:
Frequent urination, straining to urinate, and blood in the urine are some signs of urinary tract infections in pets.

Ear infections:
Signsof anear infection in pets include scratching at the ears, head shaking, and a foul odour coming from the ears.

If you notice any of these signs in your pet, it is important to take them to the veterinarian as soon as possible for proper diagnosis and treatment.

First aid and emergency care:

- Be prepared for emergencies by keeping a first aid kit and emergency supplies on hand.

- Know how to perform basic first aid, such as administering CPR and stopping bleeding.

- Contact your veterinarian or an emergency animal hospital immediately in case of an emergency.

Choosing the right veterinarian:

- Choose a veterinarian who is experienced, compassionate, and has a good rapport with your pet.

- Look for a veterinarian who is easily accessible and has convenient hours.

- Ask for recommendations from other pet owners or check online reviews.

CONCLUSION

In conclusion:

In conclusion, regular checkups and preventive care are essential for maintaining your pet's health. Common health issues can be recognised by watching for symptoms and seeking veterinary care promptly. Be prepared for emergencies by keeping a first aid kit and emergency supplies on hand, and choose a veterinarian who is experienced, compassionate, and has convenient hours. By taking care of your pet's health, you can ensure they lead a happy and healthy life.

CHAPTER 7

TRAVELING WITH PETS

Traveling with Pets

Travelingwith your pet can bea funand rewarding experience, but it requires carefulplanningand preparation. Here'swhat you need to know about traveling withyourpet.

- Before traveling, ensure your pet is up-to-date on vaccinations and has a health certificate from your veterinarian.

- Consider your pet's temperament and whether they are comfortable traveling before deciding to bring them along.

- Pack your pet's food, water, medication, and toys.

Air travel, road trips, and other modes of transportation:

- Air travel can be stressful for pets, so consult with your veterinarian before deciding to fly with your pet.

- If traveling by car, secure your pet with a seatbelt or in a crate.

- When traveling by train or bus, check the company's pet policy and book your tickets in advance.

Pet-friendly accommodations:

- Choose pet-friendly accommodations such as hotels, resorts, or rental homes that allow pets.

- Be aware of any additional fees or restrictions and ensure your pet is well-behaved.

Tips for a stress-free travel experience:

- Give your pet plenty of exercise and bathroom breaks before and during travel.

- Keep your pet's routine as consistent as possible to minimise stress.

- Consider using calming aids such as pheromone sprays or medication under the guidance of your veterinarian.

- Ensure your pet is wearing a collar with identification tags and is microchipped.

CONCLUSION

In conclusion:

In conclusion, traveling with your pet requires careful planning and preparation. Prepare for travel by ensuring your pet is up-to-date on vaccinations and packing necessary items. Consider different modes of transportation and choose pet-friendly accommodations. Make travel less stressful by giving your pet plenty of exercise and breaks, keeping their routine consistent, and using calming aids if necessary. By following these tips, you can ensure a safe and enjoyable travel experience for both you and your pet.

CHAPTER

8

PET ADOPTION
AND RESCUE

Pet Adoption and Rescue

Adopting a pet canbe a rewardingexperience, and it also provides a loving home for ananimalinneed. Here's what you need to know about pet adoption and rescue.

The benefits of adopting a pet:

- Adopting a pet can save a life and provide a loving home for an animal in need.

- Adopted pets are often already trained and socialised, making the transition to a new home easier.

- Adopting a pet can also provide companionship and emotional benefits for the owner.

Finding the right rescue organisation or shelter:

- Research local rescue organisations or shelters to find the right fit for your lifestyle and preferences.

- Look for a reputable organisation with a good track record of caring for animals and finding them loving homes.

- Ask for recommendations from other pet owners or check online reviews.

Preparing for a new pet in your home:

- Ensure your home is pet-friendly and safe by removing any hazards and providing appropriate toys and furniture.

- Purchase necessary supplies such as food, water bowls, and a bed before bringing your new pet home.

- Schedule a visit with your veterinarian to ensure your pet is up-to-date on vaccinations and to establish a healthcare plan.

Introducing your new pet to other pets and family members:

- Introduce your new pet to other pets gradually and under supervision to minimise stress and avoid conflict.

- Provide each pet with their own space and resources, such as food and water bowls, toys, and beds.

- Introduce your new pet to family members slowly and ensure they understand how to interact with the pet.

CONCLUSION

In conclusion:

In conclusion, pet adoption and rescue can provide a loving home for an animal in need and provide companionship and emotional benefits for the owner. When looking for a rescue organisation or shelter, do your research and find the right fit for your lifestyle and preferences. Prepare your home and schedule a visit with your veterinarian before bringing your new pet home. Introduce your new pet to other pets and family members gradually and under supervision to ensure a smooth transition. By adopting a pet, you can make a positive difference in their life and your own.

CONCLUSION

Getting a pet can be a wonderful addition to your life, but it is important to consider the responsibilities and commitments that come with pet ownership.

Before getting a pet, it is important to research and understand the specific needs and care requirements of the pet you are interested in. You should also ensure that you are able to provide for their basic needs, such as food, shelter, exercise, and healthcare.

Pet ownership can be rewarding and fulfilling, but it can also be challenging at times. It is important to be patient, consistent, and compassionate with your pet, and to seek out professional help if you encounter any training or behavioural issues.

By investing time and effort into properly caring for your pet, you can build a strong bond and create a happy and healthy life together.

www.ingramcontent.com/pod-product-compliance
Lightning Source LLC
Chambersburg PA
CBHW081532120626
46550CB00009B/2697